WALKING LAKELAND TRACKWAYS:
the Eastern Lakes

Mike Cresswell

Published by Sigma Leisure – an imprint of
Sigma Press, 1 South Oak Lane, Wilmslow, Cheshire SK9 6AR, England.

British Library Cataloguing in Publication Data
A CIP record for this book is available from the British Library.

ISBN: 1-85058-453-2

Typesetting and Design by: Sigma Press, Wilmslow, Cheshire.

Cover photograph: Above Tongue Gill – Walk 9 (Photo: Mike Cresswell)

Photography and maps: Mike Cresswell

Printed by: MFP Design and Print

Marching Northwards . . .

As we marched northwards towards the summit of High Street, I told my party that, since we were on a Roman road, we should speak only Latin. Our conversation dwindled to a few half-remembered Latin phrases. Then we saw approaching us from the north two groups of three soldiers in full kit, with large packs and rifles. As the first three reached us, I raised my right hand in greeting and called out, "Salvete!" They gave me a funny look. When the second group of three neared us, another member of my party asked them, "Are you centurions?" After a brief silence came the reply, "We're bloody knackered!"

Yes, the lot of a Roman legionary marching over the felltops on his way from Brocavum to Galava must have been hard (as, it would seem, is a modern soldier's). But, with this book, you can do it in stages and for pleasure - and a superb route it is.

But don't limit your ambition to being a Roman soldier: these walks enable you to be, or at least follow in the footsteps of, a Tudor traveller gazing up at the Langdale Pikes, a drover driving his cattle from Longsleddale to Ambleside, the leader of a packhorse train crossing a mountain pass, or even a highwayman or footpad seeking victims on an 18th-century turnpike.

No doubt your clothing and footwear will be more effective against cold and wet than those of your predecessors treading the dales and fells of the Lake District. And you will have a greater choice of day and route as you walk for pleasure rather than under military discipline or to earn your living. This should enable you to enjoy the beauty and excitement of this incomparable area of England. To the pleasure of the walking you can add the thrill of tracing these old and long-used transport routes, some of them still well-known and well-used, others quiet and empty. (On my two days following the Kendal-Shap turnpike on the eastern edge of the Lake District, I saw no other walker.)

You will see that some of the walks are short, easy, involve little ascent and are suitable for a day when the cloud is down on the tops, while others are long and demanding and need good weather for full appreciation. That should mean there are walks for everybody, fit and unfit, experienced or novice, and offering an introduction to the eastern Lake District, an excuse for some new walks in the area or an opportunity to return to old haunts.

There are so many old routes to be followed across Lakeland that I have chosen to limit this book to the eastern Lake District, more easily accessible by car and public transport both from within the Lake District and from surrounding areas (I have walked all these routes on day-trips using public transport from near Manchester), but I hope public demand will justify a companion volume for western Lakeland.

Now that you've read this introduction, look at the feetnotes, prepare for one of the walks, and off you go. But just be careful if you're tempted by my suggestion to become a highwayman or footpad!

Mike Cresswell

Contents

Drove Road

For Longsleddale to Ambleside, part (1), see Walk 12

Passes

Turnpikes

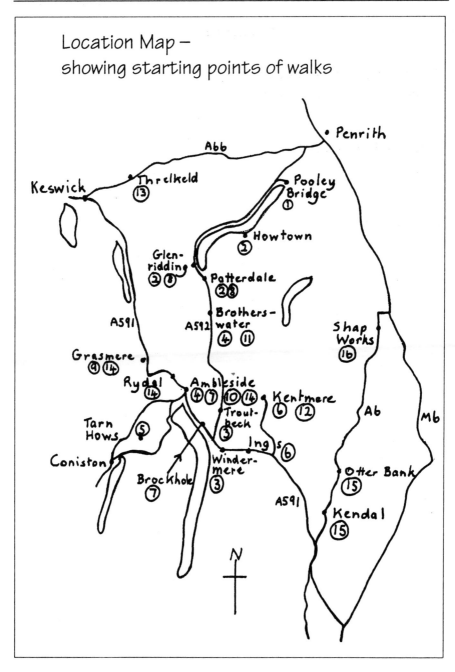

Location Map –
showing starting points of walks

Feetnotes

1. I have based the selection of routes, and the order in which they appear, on Brian Paul Hindle's book "Roads and Trackways of The Lake District", published by Moorland Publishing Co. Ltd. of Ashbourne and now out of print unfortunately, but you may be lucky enough to find a copy. Other books to which I have referred are James Southworth's "Walking the Roman Roads of Cumbria" (published by Robert Hale) and "Old Roads of Eastern Lakeland", a little book by A. Wainwright (you'll have heard of him) published by the Westmorland Gazette.

2. The location map shows the starting points of each walk, all of them west of the Lune Gorge and east of Coniston and Keswick. At the beginning of each chapter, I give the necessary information for reaching the starting points, by car and by public transport, and the relevant Ordnance Survey maps. The combination of text and sketch-map should be sufficient to direct you round each walk, but I feel it is important to carry a map as well. It makes a walk more interesting if you can identify the features around, you might stray off the route, or you might wish to cut the walk short. For the walks in this book you need, if you are to have the benefit of maps at the scale of 2½ inches to the mile, the Ordnance Survey Outdoor Leisure maps numbers 5 and 7, respectively The English Lakes North Eastern Area and The English Lakes South Eastern Area.

3. I have used public transport to reach all these walks – so I know it can be done (but they are, of course, all accessible by car too). It is important to note that the Ullswater boats do not sail all year round, that some of the bus services are restricted in the days and seasons of running and that, of course, routes and timetables can change. If in doubt, telephone the public transport enquiry line for Cumbria on 01228 812812.

4. Within the walk descriptions, I try to avoid precise distances

between features, or compass bearings or references to compass points, and I avoid timings completely. I find that all these confuse less-experienced walkers, who are so busy worrying about them that they miss the relevant instruction in the text. So I include such details only when I think they will be of particular assistance - and I assume experienced walkers can look after themselves.

5. From the walk descriptions, it will be apparent that some of the routes include steep and rough ascents and descents and exposure to felltop weather conditions, so do ensure that you are properly equipped - in every sense of the words - to tackle a particular walk on a particular day. It's worth getting into the habit of ringing the Lake District National Park Weatherline on 017687 75757 for a weather forecast and details of the felltop conditions before you set out, and be prepared to change your route to something less demanding if conditions suggest that would be wise.

6. To get the best out of the walks, you may wish to use some of the variations offered: to shorten or lengthen a walk, or to turn a circular walk into a linear one or vice versa. For instance, in Chapter 1, there are alternative first stages to the walk from Pooley Bridge and at the end you can use boat rather than feet to return to Pooley Bridge, or you can just keep going all the way along the High Street ridge for a walk of over 21 miles. There are other variations too, so I'll leave you to calculate the number of possibilities offered by that chapter alone.

7. Finally, let me recommend some background books which will add immensely to your appreciation of walks in the Lake District: "Lakeland Rocky Rambles" by Bryan Lynas, published like my book by Sigma Leisure, which describes the "geology beneath your feet" on a number of Lakeland walks including sections of some of the walks in my book; "Traditional Buildings and Life in the Lake District" by Susan Denyer, published by Victor Gollancz Ltd./Peter Crawley in association with the National Trust and, among much else, describing in words and pictures some of the buildings my walks pass; and "The Lake District Landscape Heritage", edited by William Rollinson and published by David & Charles, which includes a chapter on transport routes.

1

Roman: High Street (1)

The Route: Pooley Bridge – Winder Hall – Heughscar Hill – Arthur's Pike – Wether Hill – Fusedale – Howtown – Auterstone – Pooley Bridge

Distance: between 4 miles (with negligible ascent) and 15½ miles (with 2200 feet of ascent)

Starting point: Pooley Bridge; The English Lakes North Eastern Area map, map reference 471245

How to get there:

By car – to Pooley Bridge at the foot of Ullswater on the B5320 between Eamont Bridge (south of Penrith) and its junction with the A592 Penrith-Windermere road. There are car parks near both ends of the river-bridge.

By bus – to Pooley Bridge on the Penrith to Patterdale route.

What a magnificent excursion for 20th-century walkers the Romans devised in the 1st century A.D. when they produced their route from the fort at Brocavum just south of Penrith to Galava at the head of Windermere! The total length of the linear route I offer in this and the next two chapters is over 21 miles with more than 4000 feet of ascent, so a pretty tough day's walking.

But do not immediately give up hope of travelling in the Romans' footsteps, because I have divided the route into three circular walks within the capability of the average fell-walker, I'm sure, particularly if a boat is used – and you don't need to possess your own as, for seven months of the year, the Ullswater Navigation and Transit Company Limited will provide one for a modest fare.

This chapter, the first stage of the Roman route, takes you by pleasant field-paths north-east from Pooley Bridge to a point where the Roman track becomes walkable off roads and in open country and then turns south to begin the long climb up and along the ridge east of Ullswater, with glorious views of the lake in one direction and across the Eden valley to the Pennines in the other, with the sight of the Lakeland peaks becoming better by the minute. Beyond the stone circle called "The Cockpit", between Heughscar Hill and Arthur's Pike, I provide alternative routes, one following the Roman road reasonably closely but not always clear on the ground, and a clear path keeping nearer to the views of Ullswater.

You follow the ridge, after about 2200 feet of ascent, as far as the southern side of Wether Hill and then have an easy descent by a clear but uneroded path into Fusedale, a quiet valley which leads down to the shore of Ullswater at Howtown. If from there you catch the steamer back to Pooley Bridge, the walk would be about 11½ miles. To walk all the way back to Pooley Bridge, by a level route contouring below the ridge you have just walked, then through farmland to the lake-shore and back along by the water, would add another 4 miles to the distance. Or, if you wanted something tougher, you could combine the ridge portions of this chapter and the next, for the two ends are linked by bus and boat. Pooley Bridge to Patterdale would be 15½ miles with 3000 feet of ascent; to include the summit of High Street would add another 2 miles and 400 feet of ascent, while to finish at Glenridding would make it 1 mile more. A short cut at the beginning of the walk from Pooley Bridge would reduce the distances by a mile.

The temporarily or permanently non-energetic could just catch the boat from Pooley Bridge to Howtown and walk the 4 miles back to Pooley Bridge, very pleasant and easy but not, of course, treading any of the Roman route. Similarly you could make those 4 miles the second part of an Ullswater walk to Pooley Bridge from Patterdale or Glenridding (the first part being described in the next chapter), total lengths of 9½ or 10½ miles respectively, linking the beginning and end by bus or boat.

This is a super walk on uncrowded fells with some wonderful views; it will make you eager to sample the even-better next stage of High Street.

The Walk

From the middle of Pooley Bridge, walk along the road towards Penrith, past the church and both road junctions for Howtown. (The short cut goes up the first road to Howtown and is described later.) On the right at the second junction is Mains Farm. At the next group of buildings on the right is a double drive of gravel leading to two houses, the left-hand one being "Cracoe". Turn right to keep "Cracoe" on your left and pass a footpath sign. The Barton Centre is on your left too as you go through the gate ahead and along the track.

Follow the track near the left-hand side of the field but not into its left-hand corner; instead, make for the stile by the gate ahead and ascend the left edge of the field. Ullswater soon comes into view to the right, and the hills from wooded Dunmallard above Pooley Bridge to Helvellyn, Place Fell and Arthur's Pike were being revealed as the morning cloud broke when I last did this walk.

Climb the stile at the top of the field and bear left with the waymark, over the hummocks and making for the slight dip between two low cliffs. Then aim for the ladder-stile over the wall ahead, which you climb. But do look at another super view of Ullswater. And is the cloud off Blencathra yet, way back to the west?

Again bear slightly left with the waymark and to the left of the line of trees is a step-stile over the wall. Over that, keep by the left-hand fence with Penrith to the left and the Pennines beyond, buried in cloud.

Through the gate at the end of the field, turn right up the drive, keeping Winderhall Cottage on your right and the rest of the Winder Hall buildings on your left. What you can see of the hidden house of 1612 is handsome. You are now gently ascending the route of the Roman road.

Take the left-hand of the pair of gates, to avoid the "bull in field", and then keep parallel to the line of trees on the right, not following the more obvious track which soon bears left. Just before the last of the trees, bear left along a green path through low gorse. It heads for the cliff of Arthur's Pike dropping down to Ullswater and looking

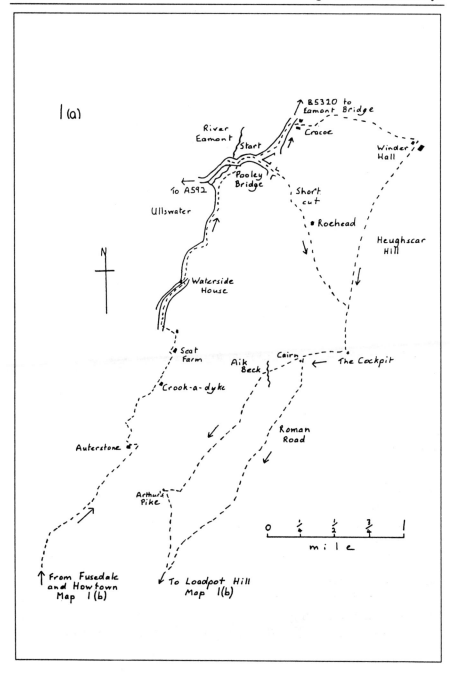

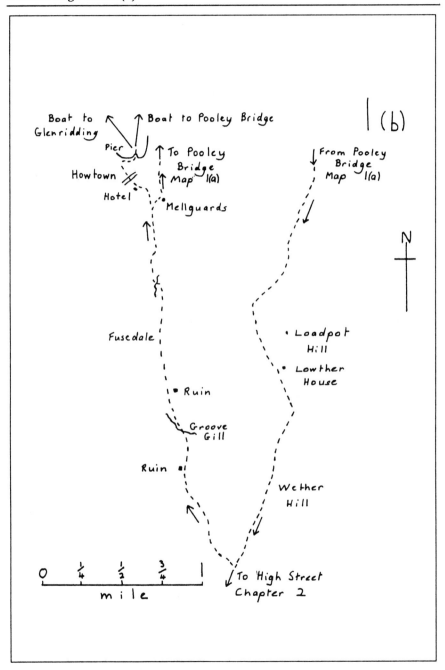

most impressive, with another stretch of the lake's length now visible. A yacht race was in helter-skelter progress on its near length.

Keep on ahead, bearing left up towards Heugh Scar, via one of the (sheep ?) paths, to join a wide track below the scar. Pooley Bridge is down to the right. At the fork by the cairn, keep on the main track and not down to the right. St. Sunday Crag looked particularly dramatic up at the head of the lake and pointed Catstycam stood proud of the cloud to the right.

The track keeps on along the hillside and then descends to a crossroads of tracks where the signpost tells you that you're on the Roman road. The track to the right leads to Pooley Bridge. (Up it come those who have taken the shorter route from Pooley Bridge, as follows: from the middle of Pooley Bridge, walk along the road towards Penrith and turn right up the road beside St. Paul's church, as though for Howtown and Martindale. When you reach the cross-roads, keep straight on, towards Roehead, and, as the road rises and curves right, Ullswater will come into view to the right. You can

"... a crossroads of tracks where the signpost tells you that you're on the Roman road ..."

look along the Helvellyn range southwards to Helvellyn itself, and to Place Fell, Hallin Fell and the cliff of Arthur's Pike on the near side of the lake. The road ends near Roehead farm, and you go through either of the gates ahead, not turning into the farm but continuing up the track on Barton Fell Common. You arrive at a crossroads of tracks beside a cairn and, even more exciting, a fingerpost which tells you that, to left and right, is the "Roman Road". Here turn right and join those who have taken the longer route from Pooley Bridge.)

Keep straight on along the Roman road and across Elder Beck to arrive at a low but impressive stone circle at The Cockpit. Here turn right and follow the well-worn path across the stream, another branch of Elder Brook, where there was a large black and gold dragonfly. Blencathra's saddleback had now appeared under the cloud.

At the fork by the cairn, make your choice between historic authenticity and views of Ullswater. To follow the route of High Street, turn left along the grassy path over marshy ground. If a fork either side of a patch of reeds comes to your notice, take the left-hand path, but you may not even notice the path to your right. Then the path climbs through rough grass and heather to a boundary stone with bench mark on a short-lived skyline. On this stretch you should be able to discern the agger, the causeway on which the Roman road was raised, with a ditch on each side. The narrow green path widens out into a track further south and then the Arthur's Pike route comes in from the right. The views on this part of the route have been of the Eden valley and the Pennines.

If, at the cairn, you decide on the Arthur's Pike route, keep straight on towards Ullswater, fording one stream and then Aik Beck in its obvious valley. Climb the far bank and then turn left up the broad green track through the bracken, round behind White Knott. It's a long, steady climb, with breath-recovery views back over Penrith. I was able to enjoy the sight of fell ponies grazing near the path, the foals keeping near to mother – and father on watchful guard.

The rocky hillock on the right is Arthur's Pike and it's worth turning right along the narrow path by the cairn for a morning coffee-stop by the cairn on the summit. There are views to the fells "back o' Blencathra" from Carrock Fell southwards, with the cleft of Mosedale obvious, to Blencathra itself (but Skiddaw was hidden in cloud), the two Mell Fells, the whole of the Helvellyn range south from Clough Head, Place Fell close at hand, magnificent St. Sunday Crag and then Fairfield and its satellites. Walk over to the cliff edge and there are even better views of Ullswater, but perhaps that's taking the diversion too far.

Then return to the track and continue uphill to the right. The hills ahead look substantial and show the need to reserve some puff for later. At the junction beyond the Pike, bear left to continue uphill and soon a green track comes from the left, the route of High Street, followed by the purists. Then you all keep on ahead and uphill.

The route passes a boundary stone and climbs beautifully gently round the right flank of Loadpot Hill (don't go over the top!), with views down to the lake at Howtown and Sandwick Bay. The heads of Fusedale and Martindale looked most attractive, and to the left of the twin peaks of Little Hart Crag I could see over the head of the Scandale Pass to the waters of what I assumed was Morecambe Bay.

Then the grooved path of the Roman route swings to the left over the crest of the ridge to the ruins of Lowther House, a former shooting-lodge. But, if you think you'll find the chimney that is illustrated in so many books about the Lake District, you're in for a great big surprise: it's gone. From the ruin, take the path to the right, leading along the ridge and down and up to Wether Hill.

Keep along the right-hand side of the ridge past Wether Hill's first breast, its cleavage, and the second breast to arrive at the corner of a wall on the right. To continue southwards along the ridge, just keep straight on and into the next chapter, but for Howtown and Pooley Bridge turn right on the near side of the wall, with views down into the Ramps Gill valley into which you are about to descend, surprisingly gently.

Keep the wall on your left and a path will come through a gateway in it. Turn right along that path, which keeps right along a shelf to descend round the face of Wether Hill. It's quite a smooth path, so perhaps you could look out at the view as you go, but it's safer to stop at intervals. The Nab is to your left and Beda Fell is across Martindale, with the Helvellyn range beyond that. Ahead are views down Martindale and across Ullswater to Blencathra.

Then the path turns left to a broken wall before following the wall to the right, and a little later it again turns left to the substantial ruin of a building. Take the path to the right of the ruin, across marshy ground and towards Ullswater. You then descend more steeply, into the head of Fusedale, to cross the sidestream, Groove Gill, on stone slabs beside a rowan tree. From there the path leads down to another ruin, beyond which you follow the clear path along the hillside, with Fusedale Beck on your left and Ullswater ahead. The fell on your left is Steel Knotts. When you reach the next sidestream, look for the plank-bridge to the right and follow the tractor-tracks beyond to continue down the dale.

Before you reach the intake wall, turn left to cross the beck by the bridge and then again follow the path down the valley until you recross the stream by the slab-bridge on the right. Now turn left down the drive from Cote Farm until you reach the cattle-grid.

(If you are catching the steamer, continue down the drive, past the Howtown Hotel, across the road, down to the shore and right to the pier. Those arriving at Howtown by boat should turn right at the landward end of the pier, left after the kissing-gate, and then go up the track and across the road to the Howtown Hotel. Keep to the left of the hotel, following the drive uphill, past an old stone bridge on the left, past the drive to Mellguards, and over a cattle-grid. Here turn left for Pooley Bridge, now with those who have descended Fusedale.)

However, if you are intending to walk to Pooley Bridge, turn right at the cattle-grid, cross the footbridge and turn left towards Mellguards, now with those walking from Patterdale or Howtown pier to Pooley Bridge. Over the stile or through the gate, turn right up the drive to the house and then left at the top gate, beside the waymark.

Only two minutes' walk is needed before you have a view of Ullswater backed by the wooded hills of Birk Crag and The Knotts, with Little Mell Fell behind. To your left is Hallin Fell, and Steel Knotts is just to your left. The pier at Howtown comes into view and to your left toy cars crawl up and down the Martindale zigzags. As I sat and watched the steamer arrive and depart, the cloud was settling lower and lower on Place Fell.

The path takes you behind a handsome farm with an enviable view and forms an easy terrace along the hillside at the foot of Bonscale Pike. The beacon on Arthur's Pike is up ahead, while down to the left Ullswater stretches away to Pooley Bridge. You keep along the foot of the open fell, above the intake wall, passing an attractive barn among trees and another that has lost its roof.

By a group of trees, you cross a bridge of slabs over Swarthbeck Gill, bounding down its attractive, twisting, bouldery course below juniper bushes. The cloud that had been on Place Fell now came down and hit me. I sheltered under trees and watched a grey steamer on a grey lake appear out of a grey distance.

Soon you see a farm down to your left before a conifer plantation, and ahead the track climbs. I suspect you don't want to ascend, so go through the gate on the left before the conifers to follow the track back to the left and down through the farm at Auterstone. Descend the curving drive from the farm until it turns left through a white gate with another farm in sight beyond. Do not go through the white gate but climb the stile ahead and turn right as instructed by one of the rocky signs.

Follow the top side of the reedy, gorsey field. Where the wall on the right bears right, you cross the boggy ground ahead to the wall corner just beyond the overhead wires and keep on with that wall on your left. Bear right along the permissive path to avoid the farm at Thwaitehill and then, at the kissing-gate on the left, go through and turn right along the track.

Keep to the left of the next farm, Crook-a-dyke, with attractive stone walling and roofing, and straight on to the wicket-gate with the white notice. Use the tremendous stepping-stone to cross the stream and follow the edge of the field to the left and then up to the right. At the end of the next field, climb the stile on the left and turn right along the field-edge. Go left in front of Seat Farm, through the gate on the right beyond it and along the walled track. The storm had now ceased and I looked back to Martindale lit dramatically below swirling clouds while sharp shafts of sunlight sought out the upper reaches of Ullswater.

Beyond the gable-end of the barn, go through the wicket-gate for Cross Dormont (there's a fingerpost), climb the stile in the field-corner and then bear left. Two stiles will take you to the left of the farm buildings at Cross Dormont. Turn left down the drive and right along the road, soon on the lake shore. At Waterside House, dated 1694 and with golden-lichened barns, turn left down the drive to the house and then to the right along the concrete drive.

Take the track near the shore, aiming for Dunmallard Hill, and then, beyond the slipway, bear left to the beach and enjoy the stormy view back. Keep along the shore, under the trees with their lake-scoured roots, occasionally looking back to fells you conquered this morning. As you near Pooley Bridge, you may be forced up onto the low cliff, a last climb, and then you see the bridge of Pooley Bridge over the River Eamont and know that there's just that last bit of track and you're in among the welcome fleshpots of the village.

The landing-stage for an aquatic return to Glenridding is over the bridge to the left. The bus for Glenridding and Patterdale stops outside the bus shelter (which offers a good place to rest your weary limbs and to cower from the rain), and the bus for Penrith leaves from opposite the shelter. But the Roman chariots don't call here any more.

2

Roman: High Street (2)

The Route: Patterdale — Howtown — Fusedale — High Raise — Straits of Riggindale — High Street — Straits of Riggindale — Angle Tarn — Patterdale

Distance: between 5½ miles (with 300 feet of ascent) and 19 miles (with 2900 feet of ascent)

Starting points:

— Glenridding; The English Lakes North Eastern Area map, map reference 387168

— Patterdale; The English Lakes North Eastern Area map, map reference 395159

— Howtown; The English Lakes North Eastern Area map, map reference 444198

How to get there:

By car — to Glenridding at the head of Ullswater on the A592 between Penrith and Windermere, park in the large car park near the information centre and walk down to the pier.

— to Patterdale 1 mile south of Glenridding on the A592 and park in the car park opposite the Patterdale Hotel.

By bus — to Glenridding on the Windermere to Glenridding (summer only) and Penrith to Patterdale routes and walk down to the pier.

— to Patterdale on the Windermere to Glenridding (summer only) and Penrith to Patterdale routes and alight near the Patterdale Hotel.

By boat — to Howtown Pier from Glenridding Pier.

Forgive me if I seem to enthuse excessively over this walk, but I had such a wonderful day the last time I did it. The early-autumn temperature was perfect, the visibility tremendous, the effect of light and shade on the fells and clouds beautiful, the panorama in every direction incredible – and I had a thrilling ornithological experience.

The best of the variations along the second stage of Roman High

Street, reaching its summit at 2718 feet, is, in my opinion, the
13½-mile route, with 2900 feet of ascent, using the boat from
Glenridding to Howtown and then walking up to the ridge via
delightful Fusedale. Then head south as far as High Street, return to
the Straits of Riggindale, and take that interesting path, in and out
above Patterdale, via Angle Tarn and Boredale Hause. It's an easy
climb to the ridge, a marvellous march along it, and a descent which
is nowhere difficult. And the views are sublime. If you omit the
there-and-back section to High Street fell itself, you save 2 miles and
400 feet of ascent, and, if you finish at Patterdale, that's a mile less.

A much harder option is to walk from Patterdale to Howtown
along the shore of Ullswater, for that adds 5½ miles to the distance.
If you have that sort of energy, you would do better, I think, to
combine this chapter and the previous one, walking from Pooley
Bridge to Patterdale, a distance of 17½ miles, and saving the lovely
lakeside walk of 9½ miles from Patterdale to Pooley Bridge (linked
by bus) for a day when you want to be leisurely. An extra mile on
that walk would enable you to complete a circle from Glenridding
by catching the steamer from Pooley Bridge at the end of the walk.
Those really in search of leisure as well as beauty could walk the
6½ miles from Glenridding, via Patterdale, to Howtown and return
by boat.

The Romans no doubt marched along the ridge in most weathers,
but you should save it for a good day and perhaps savour particularly
the view of the Helvellyn range, with Lakeland's highest fells beyond, first as you walk south along the Roman ridge and then that
same view come nearer as you return northwards above the trough
of Patterdale.

The Walk

From the car park and bus stop opposite the Patterdale Hotel, walk
along the road towards Glenridding and turn right, before the
church, along the track beside the George Starkey Hut. (If starting
to walk from Glenridding, walk south along or beside the main road
towards Patterdale and turn left beside the George Starkey Hut, just

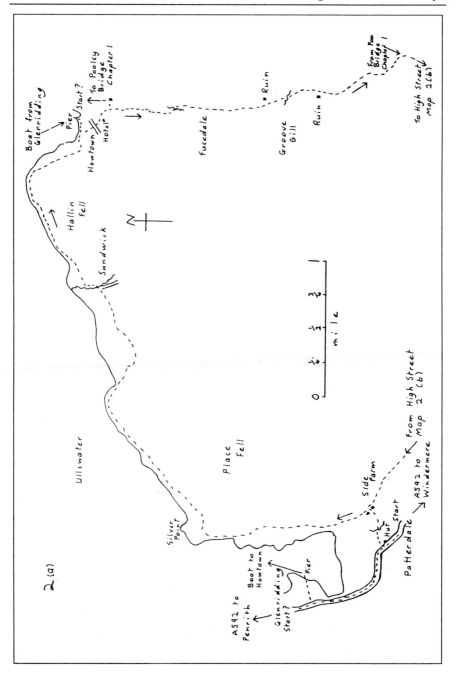

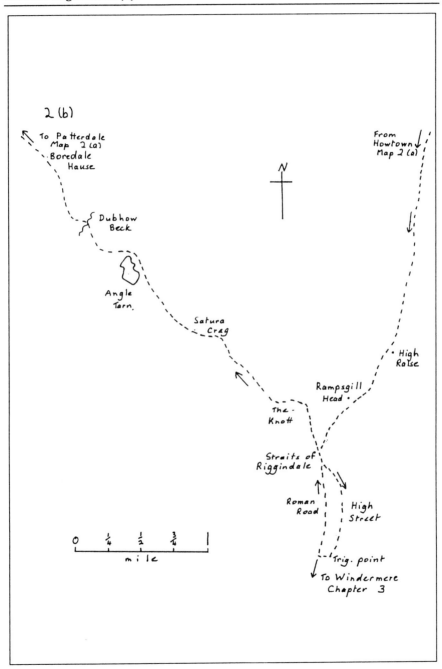

2 (b)

To Patterdale
Map 2 (a)
Boredale
House

From
Howtown
Map 2 (a)

N

Dubhow
Beck

Angle
Tarn.

Satura
Crag

High
Raise

Rampsgill
Head .

The -
Knott

Straits of
Riggindale

Roman
Road

High
Street

O   ¼   ½   ¾
      m i le

Trig. point

To Windermere
Chapter 3

beyond Patterdale church.) Cross Goldrill Beck and the valley floor to Side Farm, with its packhorses (well, ponytrekking horses, actually) and turn left as signed to Howtown.

Through the gate, you look over a crowstepped barn to Glenridding and the Greenside mine up its valley, while to their left are wooded Keldas and the clear path up to the Hole-in-the-Wall and Striding Edge. Farther left is the end of the St. Sunday Crag ridge. The track soon reveals Ullswater and you look across the lake to Glenridding with Glenridding Dodd behind it and Sheffield Pike beyond, while to the left you can look up Grisedale to Nethermost and Dollywaggon Pikes.

Keep on the track to the right of the wall. When the wall turns away to the left, stay on the main path, now wilder, rougher and more open, dropping down and then providing a fine view back to St. Sunday Crag. You pass the little island of Lingy Holm bearing a tiny tree which always makes me think, from a distance, that a heron is standing there with shoulders hunched. Then the curve of the path takes you behind Silver Point, where it's worth diverting to one of the groups of rocks on the point for a different view. On my last visit, a Howtown-bound steamer passed and a shag or cormorant flapped darkly off the water. You look across the lake to the white and grey of Glencoyne Farm.

After the point, the path swings round Silver Bay, into a juniper zone and through birch trees. Then, for those who are expecting no ascent round the lake shore, the path climbs – and you know it. A heavy shower momentarily concealed Gowbarrow Fell above Aira Force and no doubt reinforced the force before the sky was blue and white again.

Opposite Aira the path drops almost to the water's edge before climbing again to reveal Hallin Fell, Arthur's Pike and nearly to the foot of the lake. The path climbs before crossing Scalehow Beck and leaving Place Fell behind. Suddenly you are above civilised wooded fields with respectable red cattle, and you descend to the road at Sandwick. To your right you can look up the valley to the twin peaks on Beda Fell with Boredale on the near side and Martindale on the far side of its ridge. The far skyline is the High Street range.

Turn left down the road, past delightful Townhead Cottage, and, at the roundabout (!), cross the bridge on the right and follow the track on the far bank of the rushing beck. When the fingerpost instructs you, turn right on the surfaced path across the fields to Hallinhag Wood, with its beach of boulders and grey sand. Then, into the oakwood and over the roots and rocks to the roche moutonée at Kailpot Crag, from where there are good up-lake views through the tree-branches and down-lake ones to Arthur's Pike.

The path climbs through the bracken and soon curves round to the right to present a superb view to the foot of the lake, past tree-swathed Dunmallard Hill to the Pennines. White yachts sped across the briefly-blue corrugations of the lake's surface. You pass above the house of Waternook, with Howtown Wyke before you, turn left through the kissing-gate and descend the steps to the shore, to join the track to the right.

Where the track bends right, go through the kissing-gate ahead, but only if bound for the landing-stage and an immediate return by boat to Glenridding or Pooley Bridge. For Fusedale and High Street, or to reach Pooley Bridge by land, keep on the track, cross the road and go up to the Howtown Hotel. Those arriving at Howtown by boat should turn right at the landward end of the pier, left after the kissing-gate, and then go up the track and across the road to the Howtown Hotel.

Keep to the left of the hotel, following the drive uphill, past an old stone bridge on the left, past the drive to Mellguards and over a cattle-grid. Here the valley of Fusedale is revealed.

For Pooley Bridge turn left, as the sign indicates, and follow the route in the previous chapter, but for High Street follow the concrete drive towards Cote Farm. Before the drive turns left, go over the slab-bridge on the right by the waymark and then turn left to follow the path upstream through the bracken. Beyond the intake wall on the opposite bank of the beck, the path descends to the stream, crosses it by a bridge and, across the wet valley-floor, turns right up the dale again.

I disturbed a heron as I followed the line of tractor-tracks to cross a sidestream by a plank-bridge with Ullswater now visible behind. When the tractor-tracks seem to end, bear right to a clear path not far to the left of the beck. It climbs above waterfalls, gently and unmistakably, until it reaches a ruined building. Then, to escape the upper ravine of Fusedale Beck, the path bears more steeply up to the left, towards a tree on the skyline.

You ascend beside a sidestream, Groove Gill, cross it by stone slabs with rowan accompaniment, and continue uphill. The gradient eases and you emerge in the upper dale, or, more strictly, I suppose you are in the valley of Ramps Gill, one of the two branches of Martindale, almost at the level of Steel Knotts (on your left as you look back to Ullswater). To their left, and dramatic from here, are Fairfield with Cofa Pike to its right and St. Sunday Crag to the right of that. Then come Dollywaggon and Nethermost Pikes and Helvellyn.

The path is level along the hillside, across boggy ground to a more substantial ruin. From the ruin, turn uphill to the left and very soon the path swings right along the hillside to a section of high, broken wall. There it again turns up to the left aiming for the path climbing diagonally up the side of Wether Hill. To your right are the crags of Rampsgill Head which, not surprisingly, form the head of Ramps Gill, and back to the right Blencathra catches the eye. Its satellites are to the right, round to Carrock Fell, with the Mell Fells in front.

The path follows an excellent, comparatively gentle shelf up and along the fellside and then curves left towards the ridge before a fence and wall. To my right Catstycam's pointed pike looked dramatic and there are terrific views into Martindale and out to Ullswater on either side of Hallin Fell.

When the path turns right to cross a gully and go through a gateway in the wall, keep straight on up the hill for only a few more yards to reach the path along the western side of the ridge near the head of Mere Beck. Those walking the previous chapter will come along from the left, but you turn right towards High Street itself.

So, at the wall corner, turn right along by the wall and then through it. The Pennines were visible to the left and there was an impressive, cloud-topped view of the whole of the Helvellyn range to the right. You can now stride out across the peat, following the fence, if it's still there, for, as I write, the wall along the ridge is being repaired to enable the fence to be removed. Anyway, follow the western side of the ridge over the top of Red Crag, with a cairn on the right offering a good viewpoint for standing and taking in that panorama of the Helvellyn fells. Deepdale Hause looks impressive between Fairfield and St. Sunday Crag. But what is sticking up beyond it? The view through the hause changes as you proceed on the outward and homeward legs of this walk, so there is a continuing puzzle for you. The Coniston Fells are to the left of the Helvellyn range, and there is the long line of the Pennines to your left. High Raise is ahead.

Climb beside the wall and continue up the ridge. Keep straight on, but a few paces to the right just beyond the head of the gully on the right will give you a fine view down Martindale.

You arrive amazingly easily at High Raise, its cairn up to your left. I stood looking down into the valley, thinking I had never seen or heard so many ravens in one day. One came sweeping along the crags just below me. I had not realised ravens were so big; it did not "cronk" at me; it was dark red-brown, not black – wow! it was my first Lake District golden eagle.

Away to the west, Striding Edge was dramatically lit to show its narrowness. High Street was ahead with the Roman road clear up it and the tall cairn on Thornthwaite Crag to its right. To its left Mardale Ill Bell led to the Nan Bield Pass (its narrow arrête obvious) and Harter Fell. Camera and senses were working overtime.

Follow the clear path down into the depression and then take the wider, right-hand path climbing up on the far side to Rampsgill Head. Divert to the right for the full-length view of Martindale. To the west the views were of the Crinkles and the Scafells, wonderfully clear. To the north there was a glimpse of two stretches of Ullswater. Among those striking outcrops of rock is a good place for lunch: might the eagle come for crumbs?

From the summit cairns, take the worn path bearing left towards

High Street, to another spiky outcrop, where you join the path from sharp Kidsty Pike on the left. You turn right towards the Straits of Riggindale, strait indeed. A raven called on the eastern cliffs of High Street as we both looked down to Haweswater and across the ridge of Long Stile to Harter Fell.

With Riggindale on the left and the head of the Hayeswater valley ahead (good for glacial moraine), you descend to a T-junction with cairn. The route back to Patterdale and Glenridding is to the right, either immediately or after you have been to the top of High Street. I'm going left today, up to the summit, as the views are so good. That's another three-quarters of a mile or so, with 400 feet of ascent.

Purists will no doubt wish to follow the Roman route to the right of the wall, but the views on the left are better so I ascended beside the wall, looking down on Long Stile and back to Twopenny Crag. Then, as I approached the trig. point, I went across to the left-hand edge of the plateau for views of the Gatescarth Pass, almost the whole of Haweswater with the Pennines beyond, and Blea Water deep below me. I mightily annoyed ravens too; they called like hoarse, elderly, reprimanding policemen, and made a surprisingly loud noise with their wings.

The cloud was thickening above me, but to the south Windermere, the Kent Estuary and Morecambe Bay shone silver beyond the silhouette of Ill Bell and Yoke. Reluctantly I turned west to the wall and crossed beside the trig. point, beyond which was a perfect silhouette of Bowfell and the Scafells.

Beyond the wall, keep straight on downhill towards that silhouette until you meet the stony track, which is the Roman road. If you are continuing the linear walk southwards, turn left (as I wished I could, but I'd a book to write). But, if you are bound for Patterdale or Glenridding, turn right. Hayeswater is down below and the cairn on Thornthwaite Crag looks good back to the left. Back at the wall at the Straits of Riggindale, turn and look where you have just descended and you will see that you have followed a Roman-engineered shelf over the shoulder of High Street.

Go through the wall, climb to the T-junction and now, having originally come from the right, bear left with those who have omitted High Street. The broad, stony path contours round the fellside and you look down into the valley of Patterdale, with the wooded ridge of Hartsop Above How leading to Hart Crag. Round to the left, Harter Fell (the Eskdale version) fills the gap of the Wrynose Pass. Then Brotherswater comes into view.

At a cairn, the path swings peatily and soggily to the right and then, more solidly, back to the left behind The Knott. Rampsgill Head, High Raise and your morning ridge are to the right. As you descend, there is a glimpse of the blue foot of Ullswater to the north and you can see your route of ascent on the flank of Wether Hill.

Go through the wall and you can see your future route off to the right on the hummocky fells. Hartsop is ahead with Brotherswater beyond. Descend the steep, stony section of path to a junction by a cairn and there turn right in order to enjoy the yukkiness of a morass of peat. Across that, climb a little, with great views of Fairfield and Cofa Pike, Helvellyn and Catstycam over to the left.

The path follows a fence round the hillside before climbing to the rocky top of Satura Crag, a super spot. I suspect, in view of that recent floundering, that "Satura" is the tradename of the Cumbrian Saturated Peat Co. In the rocks to the left of the path are tiny tarns reflecting the blue sky and clouds, a wonderful foreground for photographs of the Helvellyn range, up Dovedale towards Dove Crag and Hart Crag, and over Hayeswater.

The enjoyably rocky path then keeps by a wall, with views to Bannerdale to the right, and arrives at an unexpected gate. Go through it and there are views to the left up Threshthwaite Cove with Caudale Moor behind, Red Screes to the right, and the Scandale Pass and twin peaks of Little Hart Crag to the right of that.

Because of its delightful shape, there are delicious moments when Angle Tarn comes into view, first from a distance and then closer. You keep above and to the right of the tarn. Beyond it, you climb again, to a corner from where there is a wonderful view of Brotherswater, shimmering in the sun, the light also catching the beck cascading down Caiston Glen beyond. And the flat floor of Patterdale is laid out map-like below you.

Round the corner, head for Blencathra. Glenridding and the head of Ullswater are there too. The now-narrow path makes its way along the steep hillside (some people might not like it) and across Dubhow Beck, and there are more, marvellous views to Red Screes and the Kirkstone Pass and across Patterdale to the silver snake of Deepdale Beck.

Then a hidden valley (pity the path's a streambed) takes you towards Place Fell. You emerge above Boredale Hause with a view to the right over Boredale, past Hallin Fell, to the foot of Ullswater, Penrith and the Pennines. To the left is a gorgeous view of the head of Ullswater.

At the walkers' crossroads of Boredale Hause, ford the stream, turn left and then take the path which bears right, aiming straight for the hotels of Patterdale village. The path swings to the right and descends along the hillside with Ullswater before and Brotherswater behind. You cross tinkling rills and then descend to the left to go through a gate and onto a tarmac drive.

Turn right through the gate and follow the bridleway down to Side Farm, left between the buildings and across Goldrill Beck to the Patterdale-Glenridding road. The car park, the bus stop for Windermere and the bus terminus for Penrith are a short distance to the left, but to walk into Glenridding turn right, past the church and, to avoid some road-walking, take the path on the left above the road soon after reaching the lake shore.

As my bus returned me to Penrith, the lake looked exquisite in the sunlight of an autumn evening, and from my southbound train I could look left to the Pennines and right to the ridge leading from Heughscar Hill to the distinctive peak of Kidsty Pike and then High Street itself – a fine end to a superb day. But most of the passengers were reading, talking or snoozing, oblivious to the view; I was tempted to ask the conductor to make an announcement instructing them to look at what they were missing.

3

Roman: High Street (3)

The Route: Windermere – Orrest Head – Troutbeck Valley – Scot Rake – Thornthwaite Crag – High Street – Thornthwaite Crag – Ill Bell – Garburn Pass – Dubbs Road – Orrest Head – Windermere

Distance: between 10½ miles (with 3000 feet of ascent) and 18½ miles (with 4200 feet of ascent)

Starting points:

– Windermere Railway Station; The English Lakes South Eastern Area map, map reference 414986

– Church Bridge, Troutbeck; The English Lakes South Eastern Area map, map reference 413027

– Limefitt Park, Troutbeck; The English Lakes South Eastern Area map, map reference 415030

(A few yards of the walk, at the summit of High Street, are on The English Lakes North Eastern Area map.)

How to get there:

By car – to Church Bridge just south of the church at Troutbeck on the A592 between Windermere and Glenridding. There is a small car park at the foot of the road leading off the A592 between the bridge and the church.

By train – to Windermere on the Oxenholme to Windermere line.

By bus – to Windermere railway station on the Bowness to Coniston, Ulverston to Ambleside, Glenridding to Windermere (summer only), Lancaster to Carlisle via Kendal and Keswick, and Grasmere to Kendal routes.

– to Limefitt Park caravan site just north of Troutbeck church on the Windermere to Glenridding route (summer only).

As the Romans continued south from the summit of High Street, which you, like them, may have reached by way of the previous chapter, which route did they take towards Windermere and their fort at Ambleside? One theory is that they descended the path of

Scot Rake from Thornthwaite Crag into the Troutbeck valley and then along the valley floor, following a track that still exists as far as Allen Knott, a couple of miles north of the town of Windermere. The other theory, with which I agree, is that they preferred to remain on high ground and then to descend gently off the southern end of the ridge south of the Garburn Pass rather than dropping into the Troutbeck valley. However, this walk accommodates both possibilities because it takes the Troutbeck valley route northwards and returns along the ridge – a superb walk full of contrasts.

The valley walk from Troutbeck is both pretty and gentle and then comes the test: 1500 feet of ascent onto the ridge at Thornthwaite Crag. Wainwright is rather dismissive of the ascent of Scot Rake: "...twentieth-century walkers will find it a long, dull ascent, with little to engage attention apart from the tracing of the Rake, which belongs more to history books than to the maps of today." Well, we're here for the history, so tracing the route is exciting, and I don't find the climb at all dull, so there!

Once you are on the ridge, the views are terrific, whether you go all the way north to the summit of High Street or immediately turn south along perhaps the most dramatic section of the whole High Street ridge, over the super little summits of Froswick and Ill Bell, their cones so distinctive when seen from a distance and not a disappointment when under your feet. From Yoke, the route is down the Garburn Road from the Garburn Pass, descending stonily back towards Troutbeck.

If you begin and end the walk at Troutbeck and do not visit the summit of High Street itself, the walk will be one of 10½ miles and 3000 feet of ascent; continuing to that summit to ensure you walk all the Roman route adds 2 miles and 400 feet of ascent. I have also provided routes from Windermere to Troutbeck and back in case you want a more demanding walk, to follow a little more of a possible Roman route or because you're using public transport and the bus to or from Troutbeck is not convenient or, if it's outside the summer period, not running. Those routes take you over Orrest Head, with its exquisite views of which Wainwright definitely approved.

The complete walk from Windermere railway station and back to Windermere would be 18½ miles and 4200 feet of ascent. To walk that extra stretch in only one direction, for example by catching the bus to Troutbeck and returning to Windermere on foot, would reduce that distance by about 3 miles and the ascent by 400 feet. Because of the difficulty of parking near Windermere railway station, I would suggest that the car-borne who wish to do almost the full walk should park at Troutbeck and follow the walk to High Street and then as far as Orrest Head before returning to Troutbeck, about 17 miles and 3800 feet of ascent, which should be sufficiently satisfying.

This walk is very much more than satisfying: it's a wonderful historical and scenic excursion, particularly on the kind of meteorologically magical day I had when I last followed this route.

The Walk

From the tourist information centre at Windermere railway station, cross the A591 to the bus shelters, turn left and then bear right up the signed path for Orrest Head. It begins as a tarmac drive winding gently uphill for, as the notice says, you've got to ascend to 784 feet. Look out for the ploughman and his horse on the weathervane to the right. At the bend beyond, you can already look well down Windermere.

After much sinuousity, the drive reaches a house and becomes rougher. Just beyond, beside a tree, the path splits, and I suggest you take the left-hand path, along by the wall, which offers more glimpses over the lake. Soon a waymark-post points you to the right, to the edge of the wood, and a view appears of the head of Windermere and its surrounding fells.

Do not climb the stile by the gate but turn right on the near side of the wall. There was a red squirrel among the trees. Climb steeply beside the wall and the toposcope on the summit of Orrest Head will be seen to the left. Benches accommodate the weary and there's another super view to the right. Now turn left through the kissing-gate between the stone plaques and up the path to the summit, a place of bare rock, seats, toposcope and that wonderful view.

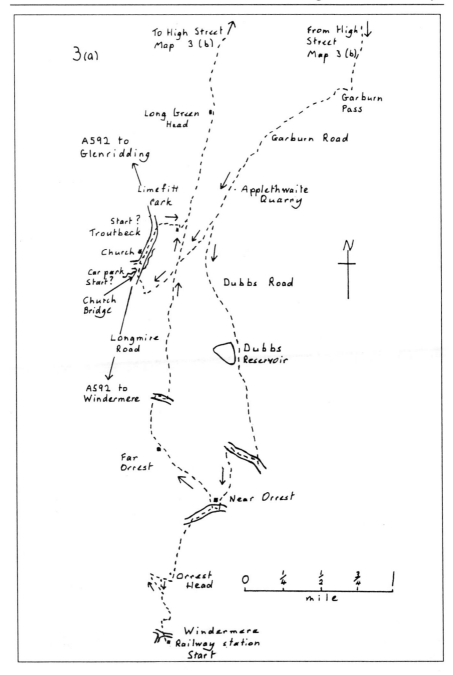

3(a)

To High Street
Map 3 (b)

From High
Street
Map 3 (b)

Garburn
Pass

Long Green
Head

A592 to
Glenridding

Garburn Road

Limefitt
Park

Applethwaite
Quarry

Start?
Troutbeck

Church

Car park
Start?

Dubbs Road

N

Church
Bridge

Longmire
Road

Dubbs
Reservoir

A592 to
Windermere

Far
Orrest

Near Orrest

Orrest
Head

0   ¼   ½   ¾   1

mile

Windermere
Railway station
Start

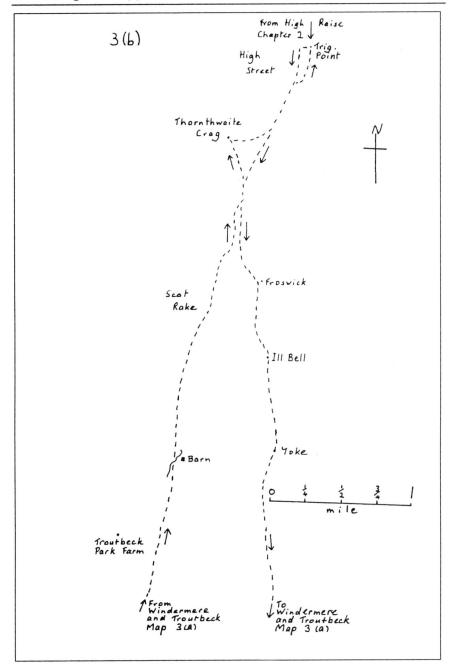

3 (b)

from High | Raise
Chapter 2 ↓

High
Street

Trig.
Point

N

Thornthwaite
Crag

Froswick

Scot
Rake

Ill Bell

Yoke

Barn

0   ¼   ½   ¾ |
mile

Troutbeck
Park Farm

From
Windermere
and Troutbeck
Map 3 (a)

To
Windermere
and Troutbeck
Map 3 (a)

When I last did this walk, the sky was grey as the cloud of a spring morning lifted and broke, offering pink and pearl-grey horizontal streaks over Morecambe Bay beyond the foot of Windermere, the cloud clearing to reveal the summit of Gummer's How at that end of the lake and forming a broken line on the golden-larched slopes of Claife Heights on the opposite shore. The summits of the Coniston range, the Crinkles, Bowfell and the Langdale Pikes were clear and black but the cloud hung low over the Fairfield fells. Wansfell Pike was almost clear but not the head of the Troutbeck valley (for which I was bound) to the right of Troutbeck village, nor Sour Howes along the ridge towards the Garburn Pass. Man intruded with the wind-turbines on the Broughton Moor skyline to the south-west. I know you've a lot more walking to do today, but try not to rush away from Orrest Head without a long look at the view.

When you do move on, continue past the toposcope and aim for the white farm, The Causeway. The grassy path descends through the bracken to the corner of the "field", you climb the step-stile, and then the path veers away from the wall on the left, to the right of two hollies and then back to the wall. Keep near the left-hand wall until you cross a stream by a slab-bridge and climb the stile by the gate ahead to reach the road.

Turn right along the road and, just before the entrance to Near Orrest Farm, climb the stile on the left, signposted to Far Orrest. Keep to the left of the farm with its old buildings and follow the waymarks along the right-hand edge of the copse and then across the next field to the white-marked stile on the left. Keep enjoying the Bowfell skyline. Now stay by the right-hand wall, past the pollarded ash, to the ladder-stile and then bear right towards the buildings of Far Orrest.

Climb the ladder-stile on the right and follow the track towards the farm. Cross the walled track via two kissing-gates and turn left to keep to the right of the farm. Beyond the farmhouse, turn left through the next kissing-gate and then right up the grassy, walled track. Where the wall on the right ends, keep on by the left-hand one, with Allen Knott up to your right and, to the left, a superb succession of views over Windermere to the Coniston fells, Bowfell and much, much more. You are now on one of the possible Roman routes.

Follow the track as it bears left through the wall and above trees which are wonderful in winter colouring, and look across to Troutbeck village stretched out along the far side of the valley.

At the road turn right and, at the first junction, left along Longmire Road, signposted to Kentmere via the Garburn Pass. The track contours comfortably along the hillside and, through a gate, a fine view is revealed ahead, up the Troutbeck valley, over Troutbeck Tongue to Thornthwaite Crag with its cairn and back along the Froswick-Ill Bell-Yoke ridge, which is your return route. Ill Bell, wreathed in cloud, looked particularly dramatic. The National Trust house of Townend can be glimpsed in Troutbeck if you know where to look and Troutbeck church also appears, in the valley bottom.

Beyond an attractive wood of larch and bracken, the track from Troutbeck to Kentmere comes in from the left. Keep straight on and then, where the Kentmere track bears right, uphill, for the Garburn Pass, bear left through the gate and along the hillside again above Limefitt Park.

If you are starting from the car park near Troutbeck church, walk left along the main road to the entrance to Limefitt Park. From the main entrance, where you may have alighted from a bus, follow the tarmac drive, with Yoke, Ill Bell, Froswick, Thornthwaite Crag and the head of the Troutbeck valley stretched out ahead. The drive takes you over Trout Beck, towards the slopes of Sour Howes and to a signposted crossroads. Keep straight on and then turn left to skirt the buildings of the Haybarn Inn. Beyond them, choose the track which bears right, uphill, to take you towards the inn and then bends sharply left through gates to lead you along the fellside away from the inn. There is a bridleway waymark. After about a hundred yards you reach the fellside track along which come those who have started from Windermere. Turn left.

The track now leads you all towards a fine panorama of Troutbeck Tongue, with Troutbeck Park farm below it and the fells set around it. Wansfell Pike and Troutbeck village are back to your left.

It's a delightfully easy walk as the path follows the foot of the fells updale, with Trout Beck in its straight course to the left and, beyond it, the Kirkstone Pass road winding round the side of Dod Hill. You descend very gradually to the farm of Long Green Head, tucked into the fellside, and, having been greeted by dogs and calves, you continue along the main track ahead, still with the wall on your left. The fells leading up via Hart Crag to Caudale Moor, snow-streaked when I was last here, are ahead to the left.

When the farm drive turns left across the valley floor, you keep straight on up the valley, with Red Screes appearing to the left and Scot Rake looking formidable up the side of Froswick before you. Your route is clear even when, abreast of Troutbeck Park farm, it reduces from track to path. It keeps beside the fellfoot wall and leads you above Hagg Gill, with glimpses of a fine waterfall, and below the spoilheaps of Park Quarry at the base of Yoke.

As you near the barn just after the quarry, turn left over the footbridge to cross the beck and climb to the gate. The northern end of the barn was being rebuilt and saved from collapse when I was last here. From the gate, you can look back to the Garburn Road descending from the pass. Continue to head up the valley, now along the foot of Troutbeck Tongue. Unfortunately the valley is too narrow for you to appreciate fully the exciting skyline of Froswick and Ill Bell, but the thrills to be found up there will be beneath your feet before too long.

Keep along the main track below the Tongue. At the fork beyond the end of the wall, take the lower, right-hand, track, through a ford and then up the valley again, now clearly climbing beside Hagg Gill. Follow the path uphill to the wicket-gate just to the left of Blue Gill descending its obvious gully. Through the gate the real climb begins, so first look back down the valley to Gummer's How near the foot of Windermere, to Troutbeck Tongue, the north end of Wansfell and the southern end of the ridge leading up to Caudale Moor on the right, and then gird your loins for the ascent; that means removing superfluous layers before the struggle.

Head up by the wall, straight on beyond it (the steepest section of the whole climb) and then left in the ascending groove of Scot Rake.

The route is clear almost everywhere, following a groove or terrace onwards and upwards along the fellside, occasionally becoming steeper where it turns more directly towards the ridge.

As you climb – fairly slowly, I suspect – you can look back to your route above Limefitt, over Troutbeck Tongue to most of the length of Windermere, and across to Coniston Old Man. Then the whole of the Coniston range is in view and Red Screes overtops the intervening ridge. After a time, on one of your halts for recovery, the summit of Ill Bell is craggily visible to the left as you look back over Windermere and you are, before too long, at the height of Threshthwaite Mouth at the head of the Troutbeck valley. The crags of Caudale Moor look impressive ahead, and behind you great expanses of Morecambe Bay lead down the Lancashire coast.

When you can see the summits of both Froswick and Ill Bell back to your right, you know you are almost on the ridge, and how splendid they looked with snow on their northern faces the last time I was here. As you turn left along the flank of the ridge, you have a glimpse through Threshthwaite Mouth of Helvellyn beyond Brotherswater. (If you don't wish to go north to High Street, you can turn back to the right along the ridge directly to the summit of Froswick.)

When you reach the plateau of Thornthwaite Crag, there is so much to see: south to Froswick, Ill Bell and Yoke and to Heysham Power Station and Blackpool Tower, and then left to the Bowland Fells, Ingleborough and the Yorkshire Dales, the Howgills, the Kentmere valley, Harter Fell and the Pennines beyond. Then comes High Street and ahead is the tall cairn on Thornthwaite Crag. Go there now and admire the cairn and the view to the west: to the very head of Windermere to the right of Wansfell, Black Combe and the Coniston Fells, Red Screes, Crinkle Crags, Bowfell, the Scafells, Great Gable and Pillar, Fairfield and the Helvellyn range with the point of Catstycam, Skiddaw and Blencathra and round to Carrock Fell, and St. Sunday Crag in front.

From the cairn, take the wide, worn path to the right, eastwards round the head of the valley containing Hayeswater and then curving left towards High Street. You are going to return along the Roman route, so on your way north keep to the right of the wall leading up to the summit and ascend gently to the trig. point, making sure you don't miss the views back down the Kentmere valley to the crags on its western side and then to the Kent estuary, seeing the river from source to sea.

At the trig. point your return route turns left through the wall, but it's worth first walking to the right to look over the crags to Blea Water and Haweswater and there may be a sheltered lunch-spot on that side of the ridge too, with the possibility of an eagle's-eye view of an eagle.

Having crossed the wall, keep straight on westwards to reach the stony path of the Roman road. There turn left after experiencing the view over Hayeswater to that wonderful panorama of fells to the west. The view south appears again, with your summit-goals of Froswick, Ill Bell and Yoke to the left and the Thornthwaite Crag cairn to the right. (You have now been joined by those walking south from the previous chapter.) You don't need to visit the cairn this time but can keep straight on and cut the corner instead of curving to the right. The peaty path – the bridleway and Roman road – stretches ahead, crosses a wet gully and climbs onto the ridge.

Then your route bears left along the fellside for views of Kentmere Reservoir and the crags on the eastern side of the ridge. You soon join the main path along the ridge and can see your outward route diverging to the right. As you descend into the dip before Froswick, there is a fine view of your morning route in the Troutbeck valley. You can, like the Romans, avoid the three summits along the ridge, but you won't be able to resist the temptation to climb them.

From the top of Froswick, you again have that view back through Threshthwaite Mouth and over Brotherswater to Helvellyn. Across on the far side of the Kentmere valley you can make out the path in Chapter 12, heading for the Nan Bield Pass, and the ridge that walk follows onto Harter Fell.

It is a steep climb up to Ill Bell and you expect a savage summit as you cross a wilderness of stone slabs, but you arrive at three very fine cairns, with tremendous views to the Pennines, the Howgills, Ingleborough, way down into Lancashire and right round the coast of Morecambe Bay, in addition to the Lakeland fells. The whole scene was made more dramatic by the dark curtains of snow showers rushing across the land-, sea- and sky-scape from the west.

Walk to the slim, southernmost cairn for a gorgeous view of the Troutbeck valley and then veer left to the path to descend to the col before Yoke, with a good view of Rainsborrow Crag, the Kentmere valley again and back to the Nan Bield Pass. Once more, like the Romans, you can avoid the summit of Yoke, but don't – because of the views back to Ill Bell from the northern end of the summit, down onto Kentmere Reservoir and up to High Street and Nan Bield.

The path passes the summit cairn and a southern one, with a good view of Windermere and a glimpse of Kentmere Tarn, and then descends, keeping to the left of an outcrop and dropping down to a wall-corner. Climb the ladder-stile there and continue along the widening ridge.

From here to the Garburn Road the ground is distinctly damp and the best advice I can give you is to keep roughly parallel to the wall on the left, seeking out visible stretches of path and trying not to get your feet wet. A drier route does bear off to the right near a stream and then south along a quarry track, but it's hardly worth seeking out. The vital task is to reach the track ahead leading from the Garburn Pass and to turn right along its unmistakeable course beside the fence.

The track, the Garburn Road, then swings left with the fence, through a gate and between walls to the right to start its sometimes-rough descent. I watched with fascinated horror as, to my right, a black storm spilled through the gap to the north of Wansfell and filled the head of the Troutbeck valley with an opaque threat, blotting out all the fells to the north. Then slowly it melted away, leaving a legacy of sunshine and shadow, and I could again see to the ridge I had just followed.

You descend to the obvious landmark of Applethwaite Quarry and its wood, pass through a wicket-gate beside a field-gate across the track and arrive at a fork above Limefitt Park. To return to Troutbeck church or Limefitt Park, take the lower track at the fork and then, at the junction by the next group of trees. bear right and continue downhill. Near the house called "The Howe", the track turns sharply back to the right and then descends steeply to the road, where you turn right for the caravan site or the car park near the church.

If, however, your destination is Windermere, at the fork below Applethwaite Quarry you take the uphill, left branch of the track to follow Dubbs Road past Dubbs Reservoir, with a succession of views to the Coniston Fells to the right. When you reach the civilised road, turn right along it, with a fine array of fells ahead. Opposite the plantation, climb the step-stile on the left beside the gate and follow the path by the right-hand wall to the corner of the field. Do not go through the gate but along by the wall to the left. Near the end of the field, climb the ladder-stile on the right, bear left through the gateway, keep straight on to the far right-hand corner of the field and climb the ladder-stile there. Bear right across the next field, keeping to the right of the stream until you cross it by a little bridge, and make for the fingerpost and step-stile in the wall ahead.

". . . follow Dubbs Road . . ."

Turn right along the road to the step-stile with fingerpost beside the gate on the left, before The Causeway farm, now back on your outward route. Over the stile, take the track as it bears right. Footbridges avoid the ford. Do not stray too far from the wall climbing on the right, keep to the left of the hollies and ascend to the right-hand corner of the field, where a stile gives access to Orrest Head. Continue up the path, forking left to the summit.

With the passage of the hours since you may have stood here this morning, the light will have changed, to render the view very different. Striking clouds enveloped Coniston Old Man but lay more lightly around the Crinkles and Bowfell, the Langdale Pikes were in shafts of sun and the head of the Troutbeck valley was a wonderful mixture of light and shade. The patterns changed by the second.

The end of the walk beckons: continue past the toposcope, through the kissing-gate and descend the path to the right beside the wall. At the white waymark beyond the iron seat, turn left and, by the wheelie-gate, keep on along the track to the left, past the house. The final stretch is the welcome gentle descent down the smooth surface of the winding drive to emerge on the main road near café, supermarket, railway station and all the other benefits of civilisation offered by urban Windermere.

4

Roman: Kirkstone Pass

The Route: Brotherswater – Hartsop Hall – Kirkstone Pass – Middle Grove – Stockghyll Force – Ambleside (– High Sweden Bridge – Scandale – Scandale Pass – Caiston Glen – Hartsop Hall – Brotherswater)

Distance: 7 miles (with 900 feet of ascent) or 10 miles or 14 miles (with 2400 feet of ascent)

Starting points:

– Cow Bridge Car Park, Brotherswater; The English Lakes North Eastern Area map, map reference 403134

– Rydal Road Car Park, Ambleside; The English Lakes South Eastern Area map, map reference 376046

– Kelsick Road, Ambleside; The English Lakes South Eastern Area map, map reference 376043

(You need both the North Eastern Area and South Eastern Area maps.)

How to get there:

By car – to Cow Bridge car park at the northern end of Brotherswater on the A592 north of the Kirkstone Pass between Windermere and Glenridding.

– to Rydal Road car park on the west side of the A591 (the road to Grasmere) just north of the town centre of Ambleside between Windermere and Grasmere.

By bus – to Cow Bridge car park at the northern end of Brotherswater between Hartsop and Patterdale on the Windermere to Glenridding route (summer only).

– to Kelsick Road in the centre of Ambleside on the Bowness to Coniston, Lancaster to Carlisle via Kendal and Keswick, Kendal to Grasmere, and Dungeon Ghyll to Ambleside routes.

There must have been many occasions when the weather was too bad to permit even the tough soldiers of the Roman army to follow their route along the High Street ridge. So they would have used the alternative route by way of Ullswater, Patterdale, the Kirkstone Pass and The Struggle to Ambleside.

The stretch of Roman road followed by this walk is described by Brian Paul Hindle in "Roads and Trackways of The Lake District" as "a massively-built man-made shelf . . . well kerbed and metalled . . . up to 24 feet wide." It provides a clear and easy ascent of the Kirkstone Pass. From the summit of the pass, at about 1500 feet, the walk follows the Roman route down The Struggle, the steep minor road to Ambleside, for a short distance before leaving the road and the Romans by taking a most attractive and enjoyable path down the valley of Stock Ghyll and along the flank of Wansfell, visiting the beck's dramatic drop over Stockghyll Force on the edge of Ambleside.

You could make this a linear walk of 7 miles from Brotherswater to Ambleside and then, in the summer, return by bus, using the frequent buses from Ambleside to Windermere railway station and then the Glenridding bus from there. Or, better still, do the bus journey first and then walk back to your car in Ambleside. But, for a really good day's walk, a circumambulation of Red Screes, you could return to Brotherswater over the Scandale Pass, using the first part of the walk in Chapter 10 and then the second part of the walk in Chapter 11 – a total length of 14 miles with 2400 feet of ascent. To make that a little easier, you could start the circuit from Ambleside instead of Brotherswater, thus avoiding the stretch in both directions between Brotherswater and the foot of Caiston Glen, to produce a walk of 10 miles, still with about 2400 feet of ascent.

The last time I walked over the Kirkstone Pass from Brotherswater to Ambleside, at the very end of November, the conditions were photogenically thrilling. Thick mist lay on the surface of Brotherswater as I began my walk, but I soon climbed above it and throughout my ascent to the Kirk Stone the pearly veil stretched down Patterdale to Ullswater. When I crossed the crest of the pass, a similar spectacle greeted me as I looked down onto distant Windermere. The mist remained there, too, throughout the day as my camera clicked its way through two films. "Would the Romans have appreciated it?" I wondered.

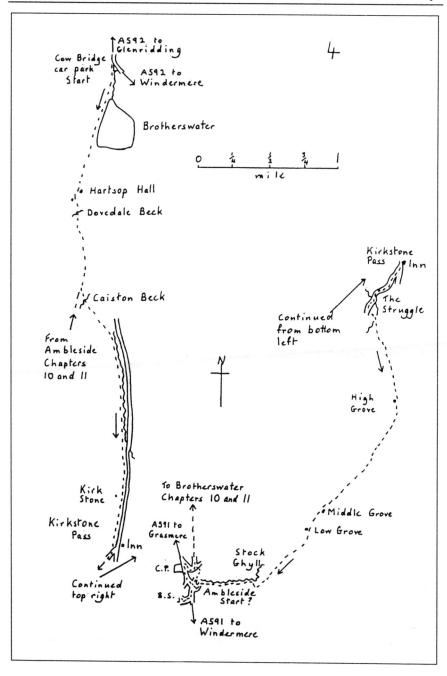

The Walk

From the main part of Cow Bridge car park, cross to the west bank of Goldrill Beck and turn left through the kissing-gate beside the instructive information board about Hartsop Hall Farm. The track leads along the oak-clad fellside of Hartsop Above How, with Goldrill Beck down to your left soon broadening out into Brotherswater. A dipper fled at my approach. You can descend to an area of flat land between track and lake and look back to Angletarn Pikes, across the water to Hartsop Dodd and ahead to Caudale Moor. But, on that memorable day when I last did this walk, there was no view up the Kirkstone Pass, my route and yours, as it was hidden by mist, in which concealed coots called.

Before the head of the lake, you have to rejoin the track and follow it past Hartsop Hall, particularly attractive from the north and often busy with sheep and dogs. Beyond, turn left and then right for a few yards before crossing the footbridge on the left with the sign for the Kirkstone and Scandale Passes. Through the wicket-gate, keep along the right-hand side of the field to the far end of the stone buildings and then turn left along the track. It leads to the left of a ridge, through it, over a bridge across Dovedale Beck and along to the right.

Across to your right now, as you approach High Hartsop Dodd, are impressive views of Dovedale and Dove Crag beyond boulders. The field has a primitive feel about it, not least when you pass between a pair of sentinel-like rocks, and the O.S. map shows it to be the site of a "Settlement".

When you arrive at a barn, go through the kissing-gate and then the right-hand gateway and along by the wall. Keep by that wall on the left and up to a bank barn, and then follow the path up through the scattered trees. The Kirkstone path diverges imperceptibly from the Scandale one shortly before you reach the kissing-gate in the wall ahead. I suggest that, when the kissing-gate comes into view, you turn left down to the wall and you should spot the footbridge across Caiston Beck not far downhill from the corner of the field. (If you have descended Caiston Glen and are wishing to return to Ambleside via the Kirkstone Pass, you should, after negotiating the kissing-gate and entering the field with the scattered trees, bear right down to the footbridge.)

Across the bridge, bear right along a path which keeps above the boggiest areas and round the foot of Middle Dodd, with views to the right up Caiston Glen. The path takes you through a broken-down section of wall and, as I climbed out of the mist, there was a wonderful view over Brotherswater to the left.

The path now heads across the hummocks of glacial moraine as it makes its way towards Kirkstone Beck and the road. The views down misty Patterdale were so marvellous that descending cars were stopping to satisfy their occupants' popping eyes and cameras.

You join an obvious terrace above Kirkstone Beck and turn up it, now on the Roman road, raised on an agger in places, eroded in others, and arriving at a stile in a cross-wall. Successors of the legionaries in the protection (or subjugation?) of Britain hurtle through the pass with a roar, apparently flying as near as possible to the surface of the Roman route. The path climbs so easily above the cascades of the beck that you won't need to keep stopping for a breather, but you must halt at intervals to look back at the view of the Roman road delineated clearly below you and to ever-lengthening Patterdale, still, on that day, floored with mist.

". . . to ever-lengthening Patterdale . . ."

A little pike below the summit of Red Screes dominates the skyline ahead on the right.

I don't know if it's the Roman engineering that does it, but the path is amazingly dry underfoot and the only stream you cross is that flowing down between Red Screes and Middle Dodd. At the next cross-wall, where the modern road crosses Kirkstone Beck, the path turns left to a stile leading out to the road. From here the Roman road is under the modern one and, for your safety and that of the traffic, I suggest you take advantage of the breached wall and the path continuing uphill to the right of the road.

As you climb, you can look back to Great Mell Fell, on the far side of Ullswater to the left of Place Fell. Beyond the first car park, the path continues to climb, to the Kirk Stone on the skyline. The stone is so appropriately named, looking like a church tower, that it is easy to identify. From there you have your final view back to the north.

Then the gradient eases, but it's boggy. As you pass below Red Screes, with St. Raven's Edge to your left, the ridge of Wansfell appears ahead, to your right is the quarry below Snarker Pike, and your gaze stretches out to Windermere. When I last did this walk, it, like Brotherswater, had a white tablecloth of mist spread across it. This veil stretched over the lowlands too, but so thinly that trees stood darkly through it.

Walk through the car park of the Kirkstone Pass Inn, "built 1496, 1500 feet above sea level", and turn right down The Struggle, the road to Ambleside which probably follows the Romans' route to Galava. Descend the Z-bend and cross Pets Bridge, over the head-stream of Stock Ghyll, to the dip beyond. There, at the footpath sign for Ambleside, turn left through the gate by the sheepfold. Cross the footbridge over Stock Ghyll and follow the clear path downstream and across sidestreams, with an impressive view back to Red Screes.

Once you are through the gateway, Windermere again appears, as does a waymark, and cairns and waymarks lead you round the hillside and towards Wansfell, as crashes and rumbles descend from the quarry.

Beyond a gateway with kissing-gate, make for the trees marking the site of High Grove and you can see your route stretching ahead along the side of Wansfell, while to the right Coniston Old Man, Wetherlam and Great Carrs appear beyond the southern ridge of Red Screes, with Black Fell in front of them and Loughrigg in front of that. The well-engineered track leads you easily along the fellside, with lovely views back up Stock Ghyll to the Kirkstone Pass and the constantly-changing vista over Windermere ahead.

You reach Middle Grove (The Grove Farm), busy and occupied. "Did you see a one-horned ram in with the sheep?" the farmer called. I didn't. From there your route is along the farm's metalled drive, past Low Grove, with Pike O' Blisco, Crinkle Crags, Bowfell and the Langdale Pikes to the right. High behind you is the white-painted Kirkstone Pass Inn. Finally Nab Scar and the whole of the western side of the Fairfield Horseshoe are across to your right.

When you reach the wood on your right, enter it by way of the turnstile and follow the path to the right, but then descend to the left to stay on the near bank of Stock Ghyll. The falls can be impressive; be careful to ensure that it is only water that falls!

After leaving Stockghyll Park at its foot, walk down the road into the centre of Ambleside. The bus stops are left and then right, while Rydal Road car park is to the right, as is the return walk to Brotherswater in Chapter 10. The Roman destination of Galava is some way beyond the town centre, on the shore of Windermere, and there are no hot baths there now, so just enjoy a pot of tea in the town.

5

1540 – 1800: Hawkshead to Little Langdale

The Route: Tarn Hows – Rose Castle – (Hawkshead Hill) – Borwick Lodge – Iron Keld Plantation – Oxen Fell High Cross – Low Arnside – Iron Keld Plantation – Tarn Hows – (Hawkshead Hill)

Distance: between 4 miles (with 400 feet of ascent) and 8 miles (with 1000 feet of ascent)

Starting points:
– Tarn Hows Car Park; The English Lakes South Eastern Area map, map reference 326996
– Hawkshead Hill; The English Lakes South Eastern Area map, map reference 338987

How to get there:
By car – to the car park at the southern end of Tarn Hows on a minor road heading north-west from Hawkshead Hill on the B5285 between Coniston and the B5286 north of Hawkshead (or follow the signposts to Tarn Hows via other routes off the B5285 and B5286.)

By bus – to Hawkshead Hill between Hawkshead and Coniston on the Bowness to Coniston via Ambleside and Hawkshead route.

Part of the "old high road" from Hawkshead to Little Langdale is now used by modern walkers on the Cumbria Way, but this chapter enables you to walk all its attractive, walled length from Borwick Lodge near the Hawkshead-Coniston road to Oxen Fell High Cross on the Skelwith Bridge-Coniston road, a distance of 2 miles. That's on the longer walks; if you take the shorter alternatives, you'll walk just over half of the old road.

All the walks take you almost all round Tarn Hows, honey-pot beauty-spot marvellous out of season. I last did this walk just before Christmas and it was very peaceful. The views are gorgeous but, on the longer walks, with an additional 600 feet of ascent, they are even

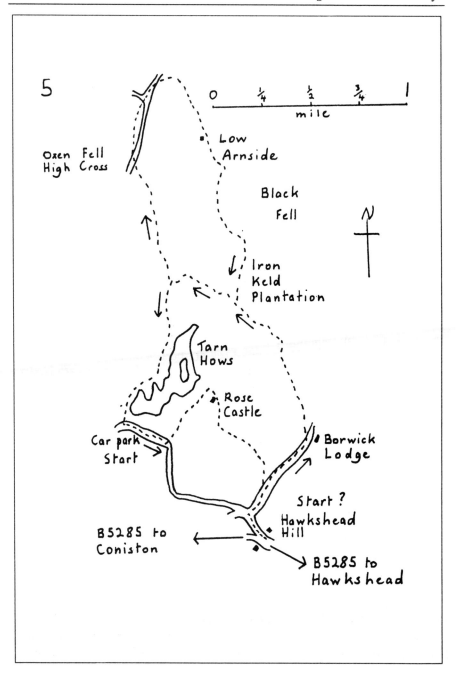

5

0   ¼   ½   ¾   1
          mile

Oxen Fell
High Cross

Low
Arnside

Black
Fell

N

Iron
Keld
Plantation

Tarn
Hows

Rose
Castle

Car park
Start

Borwick
Lodge

Start ?
Hawkshead
Hill

B5285 to
Coniston

B5285 to
Hawkshead

better (wonderful visibility and superb light and shade on that winter day) and so easily attained, even if there are some wet stretches.

The shorter walk, of 4 miles, is round Tarn Hows and along the old road, while the longer route, of 7 miles, does an additional circuit over Black Fell – and is well worth that extra effort. If you use the bus, the walk from Hawkshead Hill to the main route and back again will add a mile to the distances.

So here is a walk that will be particularly good on a winter day or summer evening when the crowds are absent and the views present.

The Walk

If starting the walk from the car park at Tarn Hows, turn right along the footpath on the tarn-side edge of the road towards Hawkshead, with a view of Wetherlam to the left, Tom Heights close at hand ahead, Red Screes peeping over Black Fell, and Froswick and Ill Bell pointed on the skyline. Very soon the Langdale Pikes appear, the Helvellyn range and the Fairfield Horseshoe.

Just before the road reaches the wood on the left, bear left up to the kissing-gate and field-gate and turn left along the broad, metalled track beside the wood and above the tarn. From the track there is a wonderful panorama from Coniston Old Man eastwards, with lovely views of Wetherlam across elegantly-shaped peninsulas and islands.

Where the track forks, keep right, uphill, and the track will curve round to the right, to the pretty stone house at Rose Castle. Go round its left-hand side to the front gate and there turn left, in the direction given by the line of stones. Now you look over Esthwaite Water to Gummer's How and the fells beyond the foot of Windermere, and there's even a hint of Morecambe Bay. Follow the path across the field, curving right and parallel to the left-hand wall to a stile in the far corner of the field's narrow end.

Over the stile, turn left, past and not over the ladder-stile, through the gate ahead and along by the right-hand wall. Windermere comes into view. At the end of the wood, the path becomes a walled track, which descends between houses and reaches the road. Walkers who began at Tarn Hows turn left along the road, while those who began and now wish to finish at Hawkshead Hill turn right along the road and left at the junction opposite Summer Hill.

Those who arrive by bus at Hawkshead Hill take the road for Tarn Hows and turn right at the first road junction by Summer Hill with its delightful summer-house. When you reach the track on the left with fingerpost, you continue along the road ahead, now with those who started at Tarn Hows. From the road there are excellent views of the south-eastern fells and of Esthwaite Water back to the right above the smoke from Hawkshead's chimneys.

Descend past Yewfield to the next road junction. Immediately beyond the junction and before Borwick Lodge, bear left up the drive which is "unsuitable for motors" but eminently suitable for walkers – the old road from Hawkshead to Little Langdale.

The track climbs gently, winding enjoyably along the hillside, with wide views to the right: to the Fairfield Horseshoe (with a

". . . winding enjoyably along the hillside . . ."

sprinkling of snow on the tops when I was last here), the twin peaks of Little Hart Crag, the whaleback of Red Screes, Caudale Moor, Thornthwaite Crag beyond Ambleside, Froswick-Ill Bell-Yoke with Wansfell in front, Windermere, Sour Howes, the fells between Kentmere and Longsleddale, and the Howgills in the distance.

You enter a juniper zone with wonderfully winter-golden grass and bracken, where Wetherlam and Coniston Old Man are impressive to the left. Then Crinkle Crags, Pike O' Blisco and Bowfell are magnificent ahead. The track begins to descend and you see on the right a bridleway fingerpost pointing into Iron Keld Plantation. For the moment stay on the main track as it bears left, but you'll come down that bridleway later if you do the longer walk.

The northern end of Tarn Hows immediately comes into view down to the left and you continue to wind downhill. At a steep, sharp bend, the larches were exquisitely golden and the bullocks bracken-brown, the Langdale Pikes were impressive to the right and Wetherlam dominant ahead.

At the bottom of the bend, go over the ladder-stile or through the gate on the left for the shorter walk; otherwise keep on along the old road, with a little tarn to the right. As you do the longer walk, look out for the bog myrtle on the left, lean over the fence, rub a leaf between your fingers and experience the delicious smell. As the track curves round to the main road, Holme Fell is craggy to your left.

When you reach the road at Oxen Fell High Cross, cross over and turn right along the footpath by the National Trust sign for Oxen Fell. Cross bridge and ladder-stile, looking ahead to Seat Sandal and Grisedale Hause, and keep by the roadside wall until another ladder-stile takes you out onto the road again. Turn left the few yards to the High Park sign and then bear right up the track with the footpath fingerpost.

The track curves round the hillside to reveal exciting views of Red Screes ahead and then left to Little Hart Crag and the Fairfield Horseshoe, Loughrigg, Silver How leading up to Blea Rigg and the Langdale Pikes, then Lingmoor and Bowfell, with the lake of Elterwater in the foreground.

Where the track forks, keep left, downhill, through the ford, and then zigzag up to the right beside the wall. On the climb, keep turning to look back at the wonderful vista, with Pike O' Blisco now in the picture in front of Crinkle Crags, Wetherlam to the left, the Helvellyn range behind Seat Sandal, and an intricately-etched coniferous foreground for contrast. Near the top of the field, go through the second gate on the left and bear right by the waymark post. Keep near the wall on the right and then bear left with the track to a fingerpost. There turn right to follow the track towards Low Arnside Farm.

Through the gateway just before the farm, fork left to keep away from it and try not to be put off by the stolid stares of the Limousin cattle with their cream-rimmed eyes. There are real calendar-views of the farm buildings with a backcloth of fells. The track twists between hummocks and across streams and rises, then keeping by a wall.

You arrive at a quiet hollow with a crag and scree on the left, leading up to the summit of Black Fell, and golden grass on its bed. As you reach the hollow, turn back to the knoll on the left to experience the view again, of Crinkle Crags revealed, and Helm Crag with its well-known rocks in the V of Dunmail Raise. Then continue beside the hollow. Might the little alcove on the right of the path be a seat for a refreshment-stop as you gaze past the larchy knoll to the distant view of the Pikes? A raven overhead cronked in agreement – or something!

As you near the wood, keep right, enter it by stile or gate and again keep right along the stony track through Iron Keld Plantation. The track contours along the hillside and, beyond another stile and gate, returns to the old road. Follow it downhill to the right for a second time and left via ladder-stile or gate at the foot of the bend to rejoin those doing the shorter walk.

The track leads to the head of Tarn Hows and you turn right along the track round the tarn. The route is between magnificent trees where, on a previous occasion, orange-peel fungus had briefly fooled me into thinking that some careless walker had cast aside the remains of his lunch. There are glimpses through the trees of the beauty of the tarn.

Cross the outflow stream from the tarn and, beyond the gate, take the broad, centre path. Where it forks, bear right and it will return you to the car park. To finish the walk at Hawkshead Hill, bear left at that fork and follow the path parallel to the road. Now turn to the beginning of the description of the walk for the route via Rose Castle to Hawkshead Hill, or, if you're in a hurry to catch a bus, the road will take you more directly to Hawkshead Hill.

6

Drove Road: Longsleddale to Ambleside (2)

The Route: Ings – Grassgarth – Whiteside End – Kentmere – Garburn Pass – Dubbs Road – Ings or Windermere

Distance: between 6 miles (with 1000 feet of ascent) and 11 miles (with 2000 feet of ascent)

Starting points:

– Ings; The English Lakes South Eastern Area map, map reference 444986

– Kentmere Church; The English Lakes South Eastern Area map, map reference 456042

How to get there:

By car– to Ings on the A591 between Kendal and Windermere and turn south off the dual carriageway to park on the old road near the church or the Watermill Inn.

By bus – to Ings between Staveley and Windermere on the Kendal to Coniston, Kendal to Ambleside, Lancaster to Carlisle via Kendal and Keswick, and Kendal to Grasmere routes.

– to Kentmere church on the Kendal to Kentmere via Staveley route (summer weekends only).

It came as rather a shock, the last time I did this walk, to descend from the train into deep, powdery snow on the platform of Staveley railway station at the beginning of a 1½-mile march along the main road to the real start of the walk at Ings. But it heralded an absolutely superb day with a white blanket covering both fells and valleys below a sky that was sometimes a completely clear blue and at other times photogenically clouded. The snow made the walk tiring, especially on the smooth, untrodden billows on the 5 miles of bridleway from Ings to Kentmere, a delightful, comparatively little-used route.

At Kentmere the walk joins the Longsleddale to Ambleside drove road over the Garburn Pass, with particularly fine views as you descend into the Troutbeck valley. Then you leave the drove road to follow another old track, Dubbs Road, southwards. To return to Ings, you've something less than 2 miles of road-walking, with pleasant views and little traffic. I enjoyed striding out along it at the end of the day, my boots covering the ground quickly compared with the earlier climb to the summit of the pass, but you could avoid that road by following part of the route in Chapter 3 so as to finish over Orrest Head and down into Windermere. That would round the day off with some lovely views and you could use the bus from Windermere railway station to Ings at the beginning or end of the day.

There are lots of possible variations on this walk: the circuit beginning and ending at Ings is 11 miles in length with 1700 feet of ascent, while to begin at Ings and end at Windermere is the same distance but the climb over Orrest Head adds another 300 feet of ascent. If you used one of the rare buses to Kentmere, it would reduce the distances by 5 miles and the ascent by 700 feet. If you wished to add the third section of the Longsleddale to Ambleside drove road described in Chapter 7 (Ings and Ambleside are linked by bus), that would be a walk of 12 miles from Ings. To walk the whole of the drove road from Longsleddale to Ambleside, you would need someone to drive you up Longsleddale to Sadgill, from where it would be 10 miles through parts of Chapters 12, 6 and 7 to Ambleside.

Even without the beauty of the snow, this is an excellent walk, passing one of my favourite Lake District buildings, Kentmere Hall with its 14th-century pele tower and gorgeous backdrop of crags, and following some fine Lakeland tracks. Oh yes, and if you think "Ings" is a mistake, looking as though someone has broken off the first part of the nameboard, it isn't and they haven't; it's from an Old Norse word meaning "water-meadows".

The Walk

If you have parked on the old road at Ings, walk along it in the Windermere direction and cross the new road to the road opposite. Or, from the bus stops at the Windermere end of the dual carriageway, go up the road on the opposite side of the bypass from the

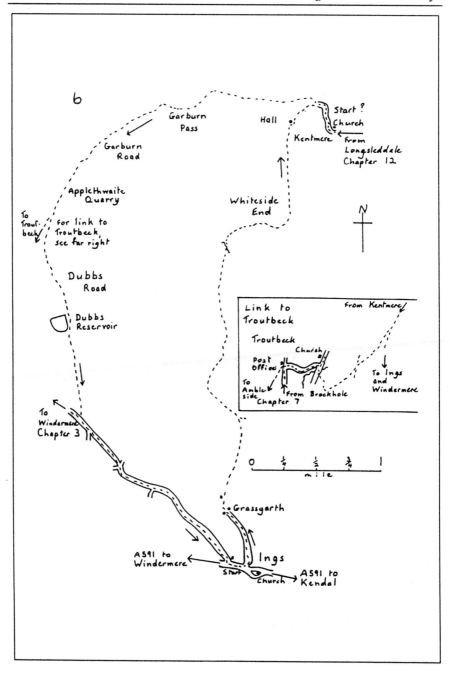

6

Garburn Pass

Garburn Road

Applethwaite Quarry

To Trout- beck

for link to Troutbeck, see far right

Dubbs Road

Dubbs Reservoir

To Windermere Chapter 3

A591 to Windermere

Hall

Kentmere

Whiteside End

Start ? Church

from Longsleddale Chapter 12

N

Link to Troutbeck

from Kentmere

Troutbeck

Post Office

Church

To Amble- side

from Brockhole

To Ings and Windermere

Chapter 7

0   ¼   ½   ¾   1
mile

Grassgarth

Ings

Start

Church

A591 to Kendal

church. The road winds gently uphill to a bench from where you can look back onto Ings church.

Keep on the road, with leftward views of the rocky, little fells on the near side of Windermere – typical hobbit-country, I feel – and wooded Claife Heights on its far side. When you reach the houses and farm at Grassgarth, follow the road to the left and up to the right, keeping to the right of St. Anne's Cottages and ignoring the footpaths to left and right. Beyond St. Anne's Farm, continue along the walled lane, now a bridleway, with Wansfell appearing to the left.

The lane leads you easily upwards to a lone tree, and then you can start succumbing to excitement at the view: to the left are Coniston Old Man and Wetherlam, Crinkle Crags, Bowfell and the Langdale Pikes, and ahead the ridge on the far side of the Kentmere valley leads via Shipman Knotts and Kentmere Pike to Harter Fell. Before the track is joined by another walled lane from the right, look over to the right to the Williamson Monument on Hugill Fell, marking the point to which Thomas Williamson, who died in 1797, used to walk every morning before breakfast.

Keep on the walled track ahead, negotiating pools in places (I had fun wetly embracing snow-covered trees in order to keep out of the water), with more views to the left, until the lane comes to an end at two gates. Go through the right-hand one and keep by the left-hand wall. Stick by that wall until it brings you to another stretch of walled lane near the end of an area of trees, with Sallows ahead. Take the walled lane to its end and then follow the right-hand wall ahead until you reach the gate ahead (not the one on the right).

Go through that gate and bear right, along the only part of the route from Ings to Kentmere where you are not guided by a wall. Keep below one trio of trees and then another, aiming for a gate ahead at a junction of walls. You have to stride across little streams but there is then a big one which defies striding. Try to find the most suitable place to ford it. I found some stepping-stones but they had a coating of snow which I did not trust and I waded through the water which was more than boot-deep; my feet soon warmed up again as I sweated through the deep snow beyond!

Pass through the gate and up by the right-hand wall ahead. It turns to the right to contour along the hillside below Whiteside End and, as you do too, you can look down the Kentmere valley. Then, with little warning, the track turns left and begins to descend. The fells leading up to Harter Fell are ahead. You can look down on Kentmere Tarn, the vestige of the much larger lake which gave its name to the valley, and then the church and village of Kentmere come into view with Raven Crag, the outlier of Yoke, on the left of the valley. I met huntsmen, hounds and terriers climbing up to the felltops, on a day when the House of Commons was debating a ban on hunting, a subject I did not raise with them.

The track descends gradually and attractively along the fellside, giving views of Kentmere church to the right but keeping Kentmere Hall hidden until almost the last moment. This is, in my opinion, the best route to approach it, descending towards it. Turn right in front of the hall, keep the concrete structures to your left, but do not go through the gateway ahead towards the church. Instead, turn left, with the concrete structures still on your left, to a wicket-gate and fingerpost on your right. Following the pointing arm uphill, make for the far top corner of the field and, through the gate there, bear right to the barn and corrugated-iron shed and along the track beside the wall on the right.

Keep between the buildings of the farm and immediately beyond them a track turns uphill to the left, signposted as a bridleway to Troutbeck. That's your route. (If you are coming from Kentmere church, continue along the road past the church and round to the left to that bridleway sign which, for you, points right, of course.)

The track is clear, curving left and then between walls. Badger Rock is the large pebble on your left and, beyond it, you can look down on Kentmere Hall and Tarn. Ahead is your ascent. There isn't a great deal to be said about the ascent except that it's up! The track is steep and rough in places and arouses sympathy for the cattle and packhorses which had to clamber up here. As you gain height, you can look back to the fells on the far side of Longsleddale and then to the Howgills, which always look wonderful under snow.

When a wall joins the track, the gradient eases and you have not far to go to the gate in the wall near the summit of the Garburn Pass.

Over the crest of the pass the snow was 2 feet deep and the light on the fells to the west was so marvellous that I failed to notice that I had left the path until I fell through the snow into an area that Wainwright describes as "abominably marshy". It was not easy to extricate my feet from snow and marsh and so they returned to their cold, wet state. But at least I got my photographs before the light changed over the Coniston Fells, wonderful on the snow and the billowing clouds above. To their right you look over Wansfell to the Crinkles, the Scafells and the Langdale Pikes, and Red Screes is the great cliff near at hand.

The track swings left with the fence, through the gate and then between walls to the right. Up to your right, the ridge leads to Yoke, and now Caudale Moor is visible at the head of the Troutbeck valley. As I aimed for Coniston Old Man, Black Combe in the far south-west of the Lake District looked amazingly close to its left. Troutbeck village and then the waters of Windermere come into sight ahead and to the right the view becomes finer with every pace as you see more of the ridge of Yoke, Ill Bell and Froswick leading up to Thornthwaite Crag.

". . . the view becomes finer with every pace . . ."

Beyond Applethwaite Quarry and its wood, you come to a wicket-gate and field-gate across the track and arrive at a fork, from where there is perhaps the best view, on this walk, of Troutbeck Tongue and the head of the Troutbeck valley, and in the opposite direction you can see Troutbeck church beyond the caravans at Limefitt Park, from which you will avert your gaze.

(To continue along the drove road to Troutbeck and Ambleside, take the lower track at the fork, at the junction by the next group of trees bear right, and continue downhill. Near the house called "The Howe", the track turns sharply back to the right and then descends steeply to the road. Turn right to cross the bridge over Trout Beck and turn left along the road before the church – well worth a visit to see the simple interior emphasising the beauty of the pre-Raphaelite east window – and up to the post office to join Chapter 7.)

To return to Ings or to finish at Windermere, however, ascend the left-hand prong of the fork, Dubbs Road. After the steepness and roughness of the Garburn Pass, the Dubbs Road, although only a track, is smooth and level. In fact, after the excitement of the previous part of the walk, it's possibly a bit flat, but there are still views back up the Troutbeck valley and you can look over Windermere to Coniston Old Man and Wetherlam. You descend to Dubbs Reservoir, across which there is a good view back to Red Screes, and then reach a road.

Here you can either turn right and follow the route in Chapter 3 to Windermere or turn left to return to Ings. From the road to Ings, you can look to the right to the Coniston Fells, with Orrest Head rather nearer. Bear left at the first fork in the road and straight on both at the staggered junction and where the lane comes in from the farm at Mislet on the right. At various points along this road there are views to the left to Red Screes, Sour Howes and Sallows and across the Kentmere valley, and to the right to Coniston Old Man.

When you see the footpath sign to Grassgarth Farm on the left (the farm was, of course, on your outward route), you know you've not far to go. The main road soon makes its presence felt and, when you reach it, Ings church and the bus stops are just a few yards to the left. There's even an "EIIR" seat, a throne indeed, on which to await your conveyance.

7

Drove Road: Longsleddale to Ambleside (3)

The Route: Brockhole – Troutbeck – Skelghyll – Ambleside

Distance: between 3½ miles and 5 miles (with 800 feet of ascent)

Starting points:

– Brockhole National Park Centre; The English Lakes South Eastern Area map, map reference 392011

– Low Fold Car Park, Ambleside; The English Lakes South Eastern Area map, map reference 376037

How to get there:

By car – to Brockhole National Park Centre on the A591 between Windermere and Ambleside (if you are visiting the centre, and you will need to catch the bus back to Brockhole from Ambleside at the end of the walk).

– to Low Fold car park in Lake Road, the A591, ½ mile south of Ambleside town centre and opposite the Log House near Hayes Garden Centre (and then catch the bus to Brockhole).

By bus – to Brockhole National Park Centre between Windermere and Ambleside on the Kendal to Coniston, Lancaster to Carlisle via Kendal and Keswick, and Bowness to Grasmere routes.

This walk provides the opportunity for a number of enjoyable activities: walking the drove road (the continuation of that from Longsleddale via Kentmere to Troutbeck) from Troutbeck to Ambleside, appreciating wonderful views down Windermere and to the fells beyond its head, looking round the National Trust house at Townend, and visiting the National Park Centre at Brockhole.

The circular walk from Ambleside, over Wansfell Pike to Troutbeck and back along the drove road via Jenkyn's Crag is so well-known and popular that I've decided on a different and easier one which utilises the frequent buses between Ambleside and Brockhole. It gently ascends the most attractive old bridleway of Wain

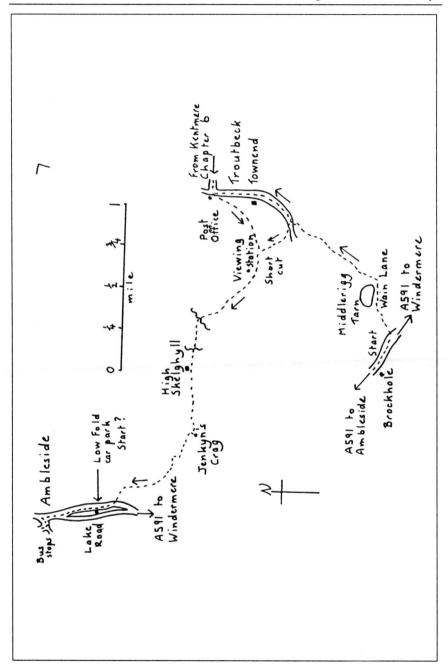

Lane and passes Townend on its way to Troutbeck before joining the better-known route westwards to Ambleside. That would be 5 miles to the centre of Ambleside (or 4½ to Low Fold car park) or you could take a short cut omitting Townend and Troutbeck for a walk of 4 miles (or 3½ to Low Fold), in all cases with a total ascent of 800 feet.

If you started the walk in the late morning, perhaps after a visit to Brockhole, you could be at Townend when it opened (afternoons only). It is a fascinating house, full of the lives of three centuries of the Browne family and on a scale that can be understood. Later in the walk, the route takes you below one of the viewing-stations appointed by the 18th-century guidebook-writer Father Thomas West, who assisted early tourists to comprehend the landscape by instructing them where and how to view the scenery – standing at the viewpoint with their back to the view and examining it in a mirror (a Claude glass) in order to see it neatly framed, captured and civilised. You have no need of such aids; you can have the views in their unconfined majesty.

The Walk

From the bus stops, which are just on the Windermere town side of Brockhole, walk towards Windermere town, past the drive for Wood Farm, and, just beyond, turn left up the bridleway of Wain Lane.

The attractive, walled lane soon leaves the busy road behind, passes a barn with crowstepped gables and one with rocky finials, and then crosses a stream by a slab-bridge beside a ford. It's delightful, as is the view to Wood Farm on the left and then, when the wall ends, across Middlerigg Tarn. The track swings round to the left and begins to climb gently, with Orrest Head to the right. Enjoy the green of the moss on the walls, the carpet of leaves underfoot, swathes of ivy (handsome in its November flowering when I last came this way) and a succession of barns – with finials, in ruins and with a datestone of 1695. As you ascend, look back and there are views up and down Windermere and across to Claife Heights.

Not long after passing between the metal gates marking the route of the Thirlmere Aqueduct carrying water to Manchester, you arrive at the road and turn right for Troutbeck. (If you wish to take the shorter route back to Ambleside, turn left up the bridleway after about 100 yards, looking back at the view down Windermere when you reach the barn and, at the T-junction, turning left and rejoining those doing the longer walk.) For Townend and Troutbeck continue along the road.

The road swings along the valley side, with Sour Howes the fell across the valley, and you can make out the Garburn Road, another stretch of the drove road you will be following to Ambleside, descending its flank from left to right. There are increasingly fine views ahead along the Yoke-Ill Bell-Froswick ridge towards Thornthwaite Crag and High Street.

The typical round chimneys of Townend appear: even if you're not going to visit it, do go up to the garden gate for the view of the house. Then pass its tremendous barn on the opposite side of the road and keep on along the west side of the Troutbeck valley until you reach the post office, perhaps for refreshments. You will have passed some of the village's many attractive houses; ahead are more, and the pubs at the northern end of Troutbeck. But your route to Ambleside turns back left at the post office and up Robin Lane – the drove road, now followed by those who have come over the Garburn Pass in the previous chapter.

You pass a trough, useful for watering animals on the route, and soon the view to the foot of Windermere is revealed in all its beauty. You reach a bench at the top of the track taken by those doing the shorter walk. Here, where they turned left, you keep straight on. All continue along the broad, walled track contouring round the hillside with that view of Windermere down to the left. When I was last here, the lake lay drab under grey cloud, but the sun must have been out to the south as the far reaches of the lake had a pink glow above them.

Do not miss the stone column of Father West's viewing-station up on the right. You can reach it via a step-stile in the wall, but the view from up there is actually no better than ones you will see from the track and path you are following.

The track takes you over a rise, the summit ridge of Wansfell is before you, and you arrive at two field-gates across the track. Go through the kissing-gate between them, signposted to Skelgill and Ambleside. And now you have the prospect across the lake and over its head to Coniston Old Man and Wetherlam and north over the Wrynose Pass to Crinkle Crags, a hint of Scafell, Bowfell and round to the Langdale Pikes.

". . . the summit ridge of Wansfell is before you . . ."

The path leads you down to a well-surfaced ford, where cattle the colour of toffee fudge were so enjoying a drink that they were reluctant to let me pass. How many generations of their forebears had drunk there as they were driven across the Lake District? You descend to the stream of Hol Beck, rushing over boulders, and turn right up the drive to High Skelghyll farm. Ten handsome, ammonite-horned tups were in the field on the right, while the ewes, no doubt the object of their desires, were in the pens above the farm.

Go through the gate into the farmyard and bear right to the gate beyond the house. That takes you into what is sometimes a pen packed tightly with sheep and difficult to force your way through to reach the gate at the far end. There you keep on along the track. On the bench before the wood, I sat spellbound, watching that pink glow down the lake turn to gold and then silver, illuminating great patches of the lake's ruffled surface, the effects created by the sun through the cloud changing with each passing moment. It was just the time and place for lunch.

I set off again, watching the few boats so late in the season and looking across to Wray Castle and Blelham Tarn. Once in the wood, you have to control your impatience at having lost the lovely views of the lake until you reach the National Trust sign for "Jenkyn's Crag" on the left. Go through the gap in the wall, up onto the rocky knoll and as far out as you dare to look over and round the cliff-side trees. You look down the lake and again out to the Coniston range and the fells beyond the head of Windermere.

Return to the track and turn left, following it as it winds downhill and taking the right-hand fork as that provides an easier descent to the bridge across the stream. On the far bank, continue downhill and soon there is a field on your left, with a view of the head of the lake, the delta of the Rivers Rothay and Brathay, over to Loughrigg Fell and up the Brathay valley to Lingmoor Fell.

As the track swings to the left, views are revealed across Ambleside to Nab Scar on the western leg of the Fairfield Horseshoe and Low Pike on the eastern leg. When the spire of Ambleside church appears like a finger beckoning you on to the end of the walk, you can look to the right up Rydale and Scandale and along the ridge towards Red Screes.

After an aerial view of Hayes Garden Centre, mecca of O.A.P.s' outings, you descend to the old Windermere-Ambleside road and turn right. After a few yards, you find on your left Low Fold car park, where you may have left your car and where buses back to Brockhole will stop. If you need to reach the centre of Ambleside, continue along the old road, which later joins Lake Road and leads you into the heart of the town.

8

Pass: Ullswater to Grasmere (1)

The Route: Glenridding (or Patterdale) – Grisedale (south side) – Ruthwaite Lodge – Grisedale Tarn – Grisedale Hause – Grisedale Tarn – Ruthwaite Lodge – Grisedale (north side) – Keldas – Glenridding

Distance: between 6½ miles (with 600 feet of ascent) and 10½ miles (with 1600 feet of ascent)

Starting points:
– Glenridding; The English Lakes North Eastern Area map, map reference 387168
– Patterdale; The English Lakes North Eastern Area map, map reference 395159
– Grisedale Bridge, Patterdale; The English Lakes North Eastern Area map, map reference 391162

How to get there:
By car– to Glenridding at the head of Ullswater on the A592 between Penrith and Windermere and park in the large car park near the information centre.
– to Patterdale 1 mile south of Glenridding and park in the car park opposite the Patterdale Hotel.

By bus– to Glenridding, Patterdale or Grisedale Bridge (between Glenridding and Patterdale) on the Windermere to Glenridding (summer only) and Penrith to Patterdale routes.

Many are the walkers who follow in Wainwright's coast-to-coast footsteps from Grasmere over Grisedale Hause to Ullswater, but this chapter and the next take you along that packhorse-route in the opposite direction and turn it, if you wish, into circular walks from Ullswater and Grasmere.

Grisedale is a magnificent valley hemmed in by the Fairfield range to the south and the Helvellyn range to the north, and with contrasting paths on each side. You follow one (the packhorse route)

outwards and return by the other. The two paths join for the real climb up past the sad spot of the Brothers' Parting to Grisedale Tarn and then further, to the summit of the pass at Grisedale Hause, at a height of almost 2000 feet, where the view changes from north-eastwards towards the Pennines to south over Morecambe Bay.

On the return to Glenridding, there is an opportunity to climb brackeny, bouldery, bluebelled, pine-dotted Keldas, definitely one of my favourite Lakeland spots with its romantic views of Ullswater and the surrounding fells. Here sepia photographs from a Victorian railway carriage become three-dimensional Technicolor, complete with "steamer" sailing down the lake.

The complete walk from Glenridding, up to Grisedale Hause, round Grisedale Tarn and back over Keldas, is about 10½ miles with 1600 feet of ascent. Omitting the circuit of the tarn reduces the distance by about ½ mile, and another ½ mile (and 200 feet of ascent) can be missed by ascending only as far as the tarn. To reach Glenridding without ascending Keldas (a gross error!) would reduce the ascent by a further 200 feet. A shorter and easier walk, avoiding much of the climb and the roughness of the upper part of Grisedale, would be one of 6½ miles and only 600 feet of ascent, starting and finishing in Patterdale and climbing only to the bridge over Ruthwaite Beck below Ruthwaite Lodge. If you are travelling by bus, the best place to alight is Grisedale Bridge, which enables you to miss the roadside walking from Glenridding or Patterdale.

The linear walk from Ullswater to Grasmere along the packhorse route would be a distance of about 8 miles, as would the journey in the opposite direction following the other legs of the two circular walks in this and the following chapter. In of summer buses link Windermere to the two ends of those walks.

Make the most of Grisedale – it's good walking – and see if I'm justified in my euphoric feelings for Keldas.

The Walk

From the car park near the information centre in Glenridding, turn right along the road towards Patterdale, past the shops with the

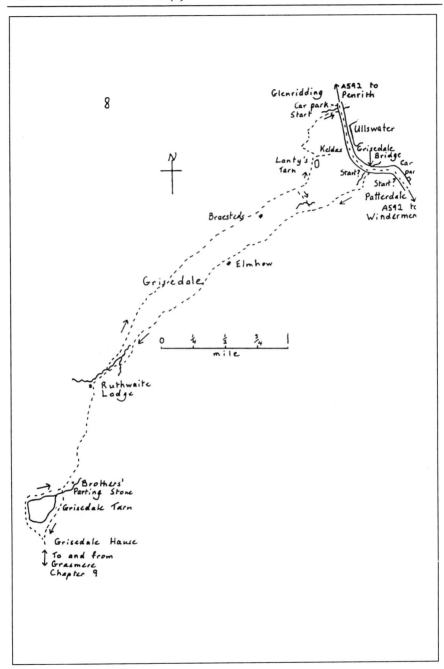

8

A541 to
Penrith

Glenridding
Car park
Start

Ullswater

Keldas

Grisedale
Bridge

Car
par

N

Lanty's
Tarn

Start?

Start?

Patterdale

A591 to
Windermere

Braesteds

Elmhow

Grisedale

0   ¼   ½   ¾   1
mile

Ruthwaite
Lodge

Brothers'
Parting Stone

Grisedale Tarn

Grisedale House

To and from
Grasmere
Chapter 9

verandah. Pass the road to the steamer pier and then, just before the road reaches the lake shore (and before St. Patrick's Well), climb the steps on the right and follow the path above the road until it rejoins the road. Now you can walk through the trees on the opposite side of the road as far as Grisedale Bridge, where the road crosses Grisedale Beck. Here you turn right up the road on the corner by the postbox.

If you have alighted from the bus at Grisedale Bridge, go up the lane between the postbox and the bridge. If you have parked your car in Patterdale, walk along the road towards Glenridding, pass the church and, where the road to Glenridding turns right, keep straight on up the minor road between the postbox and Grisedale Bridge.

Follow the minor road between the trees, past the entrance to Patterdale Hall and then uphill to the right, signposted for Grisedale and Helvellyn. Your route leads past Close Cottage, and Grisedale Beck rushes down to your right. Soon on your left is a footpath leading steeply up to Thornhow End and St. Sunday Crag.

Beyond a larch plantation, you emerge onto the flat floor of the dale. On its opposite side, the path to the Hole-in-the-Wall climbs the flank of Birkhouse Moor and leads to Striding Edge, to the left of which Nethermost Pike and Dollywaggon Pike are now revealed. Behind you is Place Fell beyond the head of Ullswater and back to your right are the pines below the summit of Keldas, on your return route.

At the junction and gate, you foresake the Helvellyn route and continue along the level track up the valley. Novice climbers are often to be found on the crags on the left, beyond which the summit of St. Sunday Crag is in view – your left-hand companion for much of the outward leg of the walk. Do not turn right across the beck to Braesteads farm but continue up the valley. The track takes you to the right of the farmhouse and outbuildings at Elmhow and then to a barn. Through the gate to its left, you continue along the line of the old packhorse track, with the white stream of Nethermostcove Beck descending, the more perceptive will be unsurprised to learn, from Nethermost Cove beneath Nethermost Pike. To its left is Eagle Crag.

After the trees of Crossing Plantation, you can see your route ascending to Ruthwaite Lodge, with Dollywaggon Pike behind. Only when you are beyond the plantation and opposite Nethermostcove Beck does the real climb begin. You've had it easy up to now. So climb the sinuousities below the little crag, with your return route obvious on the far side of the beck. Above the zigzags the gradient eases and you can enjoy the elegant cascades on Grisedale Beck, below rowan trees on which the white flowers echoed the patches of early-June snow on the crags of Dollywaggon and Nethermost.

As you cross the wooden bridge over Grisedale Beck, up to your left is the protruberance of Cofa Pike on one corner of Fairfield. From that bridge, the path bears right beside Ruthwaite Beck and brings you to a bridge over it. That is your return route down Grisedale; you could use it now if you wish to climb no further, but for Grisedale Tarn continue upwards to the left of the stream. A steepish section, with some newly-pitched lengths of path, leads up to Ruthwaite Lodge, neither a hotel nor a restaurant but perhaps a site for a refreshment-stop (if you've brought your own) and a good gaze back down Grisedale to Place Fell. A little diversion to the foot of the milky falls will be of interest, as will the relics of mining.

Now, onwards – and downwards? Yes, but only for a few feet before the track rises again, with Deepdale Hause up to your left between St. Sunday Crag and Cofa Pike. The track is rough, rocky and annoyingly deceptive, as you cannot see the top until you are almost there. Keep stopping to look at the view back down the valley to Place Fell, Ullswater and the distant Pennines. On the skyline to your left as you look back is Striding Edge.

You know you are nearing the tarn when you catch a brief glimpse of a shoulder of Seat Sandal up ahead. It disappears and you should then look out for the rock on the left, between the path and the beck, with a dark metal notice on its top. This is the Brothers' Parting Stone. Here eight lines from William Wordsworth's poem "Elegiac Verses, In Memory of My Brother, John Wordsworth" are inscribed to commemorate the parting for the last time in Grasmere of William and Dorothy, on 29th September 1800, from their brother John on his way to join his ship, subsequently lost with all hands. From here they watched him descend to Patterdale by the route you have just followed. He was followed, when I was last here, by a group of American ladies walking to Robin Hood's Bay; I lured them off the path to tell them John's story.

Just a few more feet of climbing up the path will bring Grisedale Tarn into view. If the tarn is your turning-point, make for its shore and find a spot to sit. If, however, you are intent on doing the job properly and reaching the summit of the pass, bear left across the beck's outflow from the tarn and continue to ascend above the tarn and towards the left of Seat Sandal's brooding bulk until you reach the stone wall at Grisedale Hause itself. From here you look south over Conistonwater and Morecambe Bay, but Seat Sandal blocks the view further west. If you are going to continue down to Grasmere as described in Chapter 9, you will reach the wonderful view to the west, but today you may need to redeem your car from Glenridding or Patterdale.

To do so, turn back towards Grisedale and either retrace your steps to the outflow or, for a walk round Grisedale Tarn, turn left a few paces on the tarn side of the wall and contour along the northern slope of Seat Sandal and round below Dollywaggon Pike to the head of the Grisedale path. The path round the tarn is boggy in places but does give a fine view of St. Sunday Crag across the tarn. (If you are following Chapters 9 and 8 to walk from Grasmere to Glenridding, either descend to cross Grisedale Beck where it leaves the tarn or walk left round the tarn and then arrive at the head of the path between the beck and the flank of Dollywaggon.)

Now descend that rough path to Ruthwaite Lodge. You will need to watch your feet as you descend, so stop if you wish to look at the view down Grisedale to Ullswater and the Pennines or across to St. Sunday Crag. Continue to descend steeply below Ruthwaite Lodge and then turn left across the first footbridge, over Ruthwaite Beck, (with those who ascended no further), to follow the north-west side of the valley.

As the path has now done most of its descending, it can lead you easily along the dale-side, below Eagle Crag, to a ruin, with the remains of leadmines on the fellside above. Then you cross the torrent of Nethermostcove Beck among beautifully-lichened boulders and can look back to the pikes of Cofa and Dollywaggon seemingly guarding the pass. You cross mounds of glacial moraine liberally sprinkled with massive rocks and, above Broomhill Plantation, arrive at a metal gate in a fence. I stopped just before it to sit on a convenient and sheltered rock and eat my lunch with a magnificent view back up the dale, where the route can be seen almost up to the tarn. I recommend a respite here.

As you continue along the path, you can look across the valley to the buildings of Elmhow dwarfed by St. Sunday Crag. The path rises gently above a line of Scots pines and ahead is Place Fell with the path to Boredale Hause climbing to its right. When you are above Braesteads farm, you can look back, over the hollow containing Grisedale Tarn, to Seat Sandal.

Do not descend to the farm, but keep on the rising path along the fellside, and do look back at the view of St. Sunday Crag, Dollywaggon and Nethermost Pikes and Striding Edge, with the farm nestling at the foot of the fell. After a stretch of bracken-covered hillside, the footpath from Striding Edge descends from behind to the left and you reach a wall-corner with two gates. (To return to Patterdale or for Glenridding omitting Keldas, turn through the gate on the right and descend across the beck to the track up Grisedale. Turn left along it and back to Grisedale Bridge, where you go right along the road for Patterdale and left for Glenridding.)

But, for Keldas and Glenridding, go through the kissing-gate ahead and, beyond the little stream, bear left up the path between the hawthorns and past the pines with bluebells at their feet. The path beside the wood suddenly brings you to Lanty's Tarn, an attractive pool once you have passed its concrete dam. Through the gate at the head of the tarn, you're going to bear left for Glenridding, but first, unless things are desperate, turn through the gateway on the right and uphill onto Keldas.

At the top of the first rise you could bear right up to the summit of Keldas for the view up Grisedale again, but even better is to keep straight on through the bracken and bluebells and round onto the northern side of the fell for the gorgeous views down Ullswater. The

". . . gorgeous views down Ullswater . . ."

paths have a habit of disappearing when the bracken is up and I cannot describe a precise route for you as I seem to go a slightly different way every time I'm here. Just seek out a place to sit and contemplate the delectable panorama – and finish off your food and drink.

My favourite spot (see of you can find it) is a rocky perch where some firs have fallen for it gives you an excellent buzzard's-eye view of the delta of Glenridding Beck and across to Silver Point below Place Fell, past which an Ullswater steamer was sailing when I last sat here – and an R.A.F. plane was below me too. Beyond Silver Point is Gowbarrow Fell, Great Mell Fell sticks up to its left, and then Swineside Knott leads round to Glenridding Dodd above Glenridding village. Across the glen of Glenridding is Sheffield Pike and in the valley, above the old Greenside leadworks, the track leads up to the Sticks Pass. Round to the left are Raise and Birkhouse Moor.

I was going to say that you should retrace your steps to the head of Lanty's Tarn, but a more practical instruction would be that you should "find your way" there! From the gate leading to Lanty's Tarn, turn right up the footpath, which soon descends through, when I was there in June, a stunning display of bluebells about to be swamped by the burgeoning bracken. There is a terrific view of the Glenridding (or Greenside) valley and the fells towering around it as well as of the delights of Ullswater away to your right.

At the gate, turn sharp right towards Ullswater. Through a kissing-gate, the path drops more steeply. Near the foot of the hill you come to a waymarked junction of paths: take the left-hand one, go through the gate ahead and turn right down the track past the cottages, with Keldas now up to your right. The track leads beside Glenridding Beck and into the village of Glenridding, with the bouldery backside of the National Park Information Centre on the far bank. Buses depart from across the bridge, and tea and cakes arrive in various places in the village.

9

Pass: Ullswater to Grasmere (2)

The Route: Grasmere – Tongue Gill – Grisedale Hause – Grisedale Tarn – Grisedale Hause – Little Tongue – Mill Bridge – Grasmere

Distance: between 6 miles and 8½ miles (with 2000 feet of ascent)

Starting points:

– Grasmere village; The English Lakes South Eastern Area map, map reference 337076

– Travellers Rest, Grasmere; The English Lakes South Eastern Area map, map reference 336089

(You will also need The English Lakes North Eastern Area map.)

How to get there:

By car – to Grasmere just off the A591 between Ambleside and Keswick and park in the car park off Broadgate, the B5287 leading from the centre of the village towards Keswick.

By bus – to Easedale Road in the centre of Grasmere village between Rydal and Dunmail Raise on the Kendal to Grasmere, Bowness to Grasmere, and Lancaster to Carlisle via Kendal and Keswick routes.

– to the Travellers Rest between Grasmere and Dunmail Raise on the Lancaster to Carlisle via Kendal and Keswick route.

The second stage of the packhorse route from Ullswater to Grasmere over Grisedale Hause gives most beautiful views from the slopes of Seat Sandal on a path which sidles round the fell before a gorgeously-grassy descent towards Grasmere. And, with a little searching, you can find a virtually-unused zigzag, shown as the right of way on the Ordnance Survey map but not referred to by Wainwright in his "The Eastern Fells". It avoids a steep section of the modern, much-used path.

It's the walk's descending return to Grasmere which follows the old packhorse route on open fell with wide views, in contrast to the outward route up the valley of Tongue Gill. At the highest part of the walk, and of the pass, you cross Grisedale Hause and drop down to the glaciated bowl of Grisedale Tarn, where a circuit of the tarn offers another selection of views.

If you park in the centre of Grasmere or catch the bus to and from the village, the walk will be one of 8½ miles, but you could reduce the distance to 6 miles by catching the bus to the Travellers Rest and back from Mill Bridge on the main road north of Grasmere. As Grasmere would be a better place to wait for a bus at the end of the day, and because it would be a pity to miss the excellent views back to Grisedale Hause from the quiet road between Mill Bridge and Grasmere, I recommend you to walk back into Grasmere even if you caught the bus out to the Travellers Rest; that would be a walk of 7½ miles. In all cases there would be a climb of about 2000 feet. (It would be possible to reduce both distance and ascent by turning back for home as soon as the outward route meets the return one above Tongue Gill, but I have assumed that, with Grisedale Hause and Tarn then so close, you will want to go the whole hog – a very appropriate expression since "Grisedale" means "the valley of the pigs"!)

If you wish to combine the outward route in this chapter with the return route in Chapter 8 for a linear walk from Grasmere to Glenridding (only incidentally following short stretches of the pack-horse route) or to follow the whole of the packhorse route from Glenridding or Patterdale to Grasmere by adding the outward route in Chapter 8 to the return route in this chapter, you can link the two ends of those walks by using buses from Windermere; for more detail, see the previous chapter.

Walk this chapter on a fine day and the views as you round the flank of Seat Sandal will long remain in your mind's eye.

The Walk

From the bus stops near the end of Easedale Road, walk along Broadgate towards Keswick, or from the Broadgate car park turn right towards Keswick. Stone Arthur and Seat Sandal are up ahead

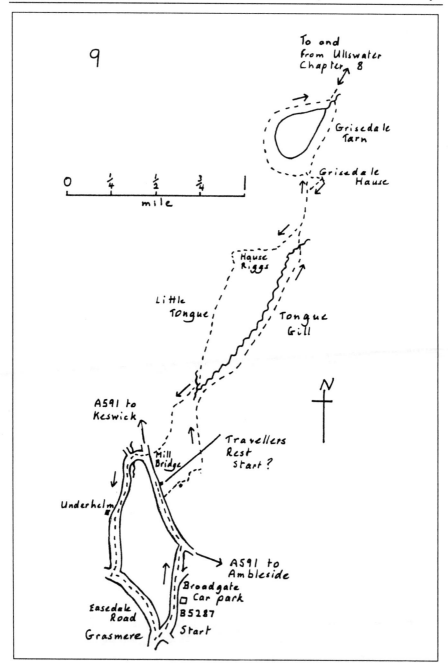

9

To and
from Ullswater
Chapter 8

Grisedale
Tarn

Grisedale
Hause

0   ¼   ½   ¾
mile

Hause
Riggs

Little
Tongue

Tongue
Gill

A591 to
Keswick

N

Mill
Bridge

Travellers
Rest?
Start?

Underhelm

A591 to
Ambleside

Broadgate
Car park

Easedale
Road
Grasmere

B5287

Start

and Helm Crag and Steel Fell to the left. After crossing the bridge over the River Rothay, bear left along Pye Lane and up to the main road. There turn left, again towards Keswick, with Silver How and Blea Rigg back to your left.

Just before the Travellers Rest, turn right up the signed footpath which is also the drive to Meadow Brow. (If you have alighted from a bus at the Travellers Rest, walk down the road towards Grasmere and turn left up the drive.) The path follows the drive to the left of the house, beside Stone Arthur Cottage, and then to the right across the field and through the gateway before swinging round to the left to another gateway, with a fine view up the Greenburn valley.

Just beyond that gate, turn up the path – it's waymarked – to a gateway in the top wall. From there you have a good view back over Grasmere village and lake. Now go through the adjacent kissing-gate and turn left along the hillside to enjoy looking out to Helm Crag and the Gibson Knott ridge beyond, up the Greenburn valley and round to Steel Fell to the left of Dunmail Raise. Just to the left of Helm Crag is a glimpse of Harrison Stickle and then Blea Rigg and Silver How lead back to Grasmere and Loughrigg Fell.

The path remains almost level between walls and along the hillside. Down to your left, beyond Tongue Gill, is your return route to Grasmere. You round a corner of Great Rigg and ahead are Seat Sandal and Fairfield with your outward and return routes passing between them. Your return route is the clearly-visible green path descending Little Tongue to the left of both Tongue Gill and Little Tongue Gill and becoming a track.

Having walked through the sheep-pen, comply with the waymark and keep to the left of the wall on the right. Don't lose height by descending to the lower path but keep well above the stream and then above the wall, soon with views back to Great and Little Carrs in the Coniston range and to the Old Lady Playing the Organ on Helm Crag. The climb is quite gentle and you have retrospective views to Wetherlam and Swirl How, to Pike O' Blisco, and to Harrison Stickle and Pavey Ark. Of course, that gentleness of ascent can't last forever and you can see the steep stretch ahead, beyond a cairn. But the path is well stone-pitched in places, in others on naked rock, and you can now look back to the Crinkles. Just when you need a rest, you cross Tongue Gill in a pleasant spot below a cascade where it drops down from the hanging valley of Hause Moss, an excellent excuse for a stop.

After a further short stretch of steep pitching, a path comes in from the left just before you cross a stream in a wide stone gully; that path back to the left is your return route, the old packhorse track. From the junction, you have a glimpse of Conistonwater.

For Grisedale Tarn, continue upwards. When the path levels out, with several cairns, look to the right ahead and see if you can discern a shelf slanting down to the right from just below the lowest point on the skyline and extending almost to the stream-course on the right. That is the zig of the packhorses' zigzag which I hope you will be able to follow on your return to Grasmere. In this direction, however, keep on up the pitched path but try to see where the packhorse rake rejoins the path, near where the gradient eases, to make spotting it simpler on your return.

Soon you reach the wall at Grisedale Hause, the head of the pass, with more of Conistonwater visible and Morecambe Bay beyond. Once through the wall, you look over Grisedale Tarn to Dollywaggon Pike and to the left, between Dollywaggon and Seat Sandal, are Grisedale Pike and Hobcarton Pike.

You could now continue along the path to a lunch-spot near the outflow from the tarn, but I suggest you turn left along the path on the northern flank of Seat Sandal for a circumambulation of the tarn, boggy though the path is in places. A few paces along that path provide a view down Grisedale to Ullswater with the Pennines beyond and the pointed peak of Place Fell to the left of the elegant ridge leading to St. Sunday Crag. As the path makes its way round the tarn, the view across the water becomes impressive as the ridge from St. Sunday Crag descends to Deepdale Hause and then climbs again to Cofa Pike and Fairfield, while, to the left, Scafell Pike, Great End, Glaramara and Great Gable come into sight between Seat Sandal and Dollywaggon. As you will become aware for yourself, there is sogginess below Dollywaggon.

The path brings you round to rocky peninsulas, hummocks and beaches where you should be able to find a sheltered spot for lunch even though this hollow in the hills is almost always draughty – and the home of importunate mallard.

Continue round the tarn, over its outflow stream of Grisedale Beck, and up the path to the right to climb again to the hause, now with those who have walked from Ullswater in the previous chapter. As you look down onto the tarn, you can almost feel the ice grinding out its cavity, can't you? And on the slope of Dollywaggon Pike you can see how the old zigzags of the Victorian tourists' pony track have been mutilated by impatient walkers.

Back at the summit of the pass, you can begin to appreciate the view southwards again to Morecambe Bay. As you descend, remember that you're looking for the packhorse route turning off to the left. It's about 30 paces below a stone drainage channel across the path, descends to the left and is about 4 feet wide. If you find it, try it; if you don't, fear not and descend the pitched path. Once on the old route, you should have no difficulty in following it down and along the hillside (there's one soggy bit) to just below a pointed rock, where the track clearly curves back to the right, as you now do. Then the route becomes obscure, but keep on along the fellside towards the stone-pitched path, descending a little but avoiding the boggy floor of this hanging valley. You rejoin the obvious path by a group of cairns, having avoided its steepest stretch.

The path begins to descend again on stone pitching and brings you to a fork immediately after a wide drainage channel. Your route up out of Grasmere was the pitched path descending to the left, but for your return you take the old packhorse route along the fellside to the right. You look down on your outward route and its waterfalls and across to the slopes of Great Rigg and Heron Pike as you mount gently round the fellside of Seat Sandal. Then you come round a corner and look down on Grasmere, Silver How and Helm Crag and across to Morecambe Bay, Conistonwater, the Coniston Fells with Lingmoor in front, Pike O' Blisco and the Crinkles beyond Blea Rigg, and the Langdale Pikes with Bowfell behind them. The contrast between the valley in the foreground and the fells beyond is highly photogenic.

The path remains for as long as possible along the top of the line of low crags, Hause Riggs, descends stonily along the hillside and then becomes a grassy rake like that used earlier. You are aiming for the track down the valley of Little Tongue Gill but see if you can follow the green zigzags which eased the passage of the packhorses down the upper part of Little Tongue. As you descend the comfortably-short grass on the nose of the tongue (work that one out!), you can keep looking at the scene ahead or, as I always seem able to do, you can sit and bask in the afternoon sun for a tea-stop with panorama.

As you cross Little Tongue Gill, the path becomes a track and you continue down it, across Tongue Gill, past a sheepfold, and then above Tongue Gill. From the track descending to the main road, there are good views of the beck below you, up the Greenburn valley and down onto the flat floor of the Vale of Grasmere – and don't miss the Coast-to-Coast sign on the first house on the left.

If you are not catching a bus here at Mill Bridge, cross the main road with extreme care and take the quiet road opposite, past the

". . . above Tongue Gill . . ."

old mill and down to Low Mill Bridge across the Rothay. There turn left along the road, which rises a little and offers a selection of views: ahead to Silver How and then, swinging round to the left, to Loughrigg and the ridge leading up to Great Rigg, Stone Arthur and, best of all, Fairfield and Seat Sandal with Grisedale Hause, Great and Little Tongues and your return route. And below Stone Arthur you can see your outward route, especially the level length between the walls.

Beyond the farm at Underhelm, the view back to Grisedale Hause is even better – and tiny lambs may rush to the fence to suck your fingers if their nanny-goat nannies are not looking. Follow the road down to the T-junction and then left into Grasmere to arrive at the junction of Easedale Road and Broadgate, with bus stops to left and right, the Broadgate car park to the left – and the route to the gingerbread shop straight ahead.

10

Pass: Scandale Pass (1)

The Route: Ambleside – High Sweden Bridge – Scandale – Scandale Pass – Red Screes – Snarker Pike – Ambleside

Distance: 8 miles (with 2400 feet of ascent)

Starting points:

– Rydal Road Car Park, Ambleside; The English Lakes South Eastern Area map, map reference 376046

– Kelsick Road, Ambleside; The English Lakes South Eastern Area map, map reference 376043

How to get there:

By car – to the Rydal Road car park on the west side of the A591 (the road to Grasmere) just north of the town centre of Ambleside between Windermere and Grasmere.

By bus – to Kelsick Road in the centre of Ambleside on the Bowness to Coniston, Lancaster to Carlisle via Kendal and Keswick, Kendal to Grasmere, and Dungeon Ghyll to Ambleside routes.

The ascent to the Scandale Pass provides you with an excellent excuse to walk one of my favourite routes for the shorter days of the year – from Ambleside up Scandale to the pass and then to the summit of Red Screes, a wonderful viewpoint, and down its southern ridge back to Ambleside, a walk of 8 miles with 2400 feet of ascent. Or, by continuing into the next chapter, the walk to the pass can be the first section of the 7-mile journey (with an ascent of 1600 feet) to Brotherswater in Patterdale (the route real travellers would have taken). From there, you could either return by bus to Ambleside via Windermere if you choose the right time of year or, before reaching Brotherswater, you could, if feeling energetic, turn south and ascend the Roman road through the Kirkstone Pass and then by

Stock Ghyll back to Ambleside, as described in Chapter 4, a total circuit of 10 miles and about 2400 feet of ascent.

Because the Kirkstone Pass is easier and a little lower than the Scandale Pass, it has always been used more than Scandale. That is still the case and can be clearly seen as you stand on the summit of Red Screes and compare the number of walkers you saw in Scandale with the number of vehicles crawling up to the Kirk Stone.

Scandale is peaceful, High Sweden Bridge is a beautiful spot near its foot, the views from the summit of Red Screes are tremendous in all directions, both over the fells and south to Windermere and Morecambe Bay, and the descent towards lake and sea is a delight. Those views were particularly dramatic one day in snow with further snowclouds rushing at me from the north. Be careful if you are doing this walk in winter conditions and don't do it unless you can have the views. They really are good – without too much effort.

The Walk

From the bus stops in Kelsick Road, walk uphill with the County Library on your right, to the main street. Turn left, past the book shop (for yet another copy of this superb book?), past the Queens Hotel and over the road to the market cross. Bear right along North Road by the cross, over Stock Ghyll and immediately up the path on the right, Peggy Hill. At the junction, bear right, passing the house called "Shepherd's Fold", and then the road swings left and up to the old parish church. Turn left, to keep the church on your right and to arrive at benches – not yet needed as a seat but perhaps a good spot for removing the first layer of excess clothing. Back to your left is the early 17th-century farmhouse of How Head, with "wrostler" or "wrestler" slates embracing each other like Cumbrian wrestlers along the ridges of the roof. Cross the road, the foot of "The Struggle", to Sweden Bridge Lane.

Walkers starting from the Rydal Road car park should leave it by the vehicular route, turn right and then bear left up Smithy Brow and Kirkstone Road until they reach the pair of benches and turn left into Sweden Bridge Lane.

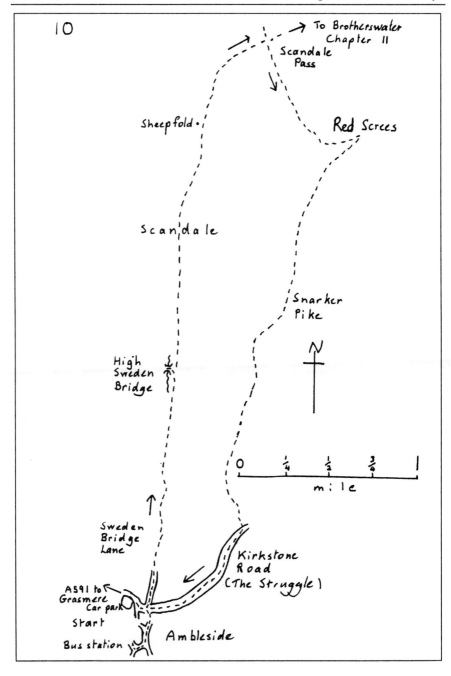

10

To Brotherswater
Chapter 11

Scandale Pass

Sheep fold •

Red Screes

Scandale

Snarker Pike

N

High Sweden Bridge

0 ¼ ½ ¾ 1

mile

Sweden Bridge Lane

Kirkstone Road (The Struggle)

A591 to Grasmere
Car park

Start

Bus station

Ambleside

Follow Sweden Bridge Lane uphill and, where it forks, keep with Sweden Bridge Lane and through the gate ahead. Beyond it the road becomes a track and marvellous views begin. From a gate on the left after about 100 yards, you can look over Loughrigg Fell to Coniston Old Man, Bowfell and the Langdale Pikes, and to Nab Scar and Great Rigg on one side of the Fairfield Horseshoe and High and Low Pikes on its other side. To the right of the path is Wansfell and behind you Windermere appears.

Even while enjoying the views to the left, try not to miss on the right an excellent example of a pair of gate stoups complete with poles. Then Rydal Water appears to the left and Crinkle Crags to the left of Bowfell.

As the track takes you into Rough Sides Wood and through another gate, there rises the roar of Scandale Beck, tumbling down from the hanging valley of Scandale. Unfortunately the falls are largely hidden in the beck's chasm. Then, when you emerge from the trees, High Pike dominates the view and, when I last did this walk, the golden bracken burst into sight as I came out into sunshine from sylvan shade.

At the fork in the track, the delightful little High Sweden Bridge appears, a packhorse bridge of the 17th or 18th century. "Sweden", incidentally, refers to land cleared of trees by burning. Your route is to the right and not over the bridge, but it's too good a spot not to take a closer view and a photograph, and perhaps to have an early coffee-stop.

Then return to the junction of tracks and turn left up Scandale. Soon the track becomes walled on both sides, the beck is rushing on your left, and there are views back over Windermere to Claife Heights. Now you have an easy stretch of walking, gently rising and falling beneath Low and High Pikes, with the Red Screes ridge on your right and the fine cairn on High Bakestones ahead.

When you reach the one and a half larch trees on the right, you can see your route ahead: between the walls, up through the bracken beside the single wall and then climbing to the right below the twin peaks of Little Hart Crag and up to the lowest point on the skyline.

". . . the delightful little High Sweden Bridge appears . . ."

From there you either drop down over the skyline for Patterdale or, for Red Screes, turn back to the right and up the skyline. Easy, isn't it? We'll see.

As you near the gate at the end of the paired walls, you will realise how flat the route now is and you notice the U-shaped profile of the valley – a classic example of glaciation. Beyond the gate you become very conscious of streams crossing the floor of Scandale Bottom and requiring to be forded, one in particular demanding care in wet periods. Beyond them you keep to the left of the wall and then past a compartmentalised sheepfold (useful with mixed parties of walkers for separating tups and yows for a comfort-stop) to a gate. Here the real climb begins.

Through the gate, first keep near the wall and then follow the path, rough in places but now less steep, up to the right. Gradually the view back to Windermere is replaced by one of Coniston Old Man to the right of Low Pike and Morecambe Bay to its left.

At the crest of the pass, with a view ahead to the rough slopes of Caudale Moor and beyond to the High Street ridge, climb the ladder-stile. If you're descending to Patterdale, bear right to the little cairn and then bear left to follow the path along the right-hand side of the hummock. From there the route, described in Chapter 11, is clear.

However, to ascend Red Screes, having climbed the ladder-stile turn right, up by the wall. The path climbs gently at first, over rock slabs, but then more steeply, twisting and turning by the wall. The views improve with every foot of ascent: to the right the whole of the Coniston range with Harter Fell through the Wrynose Pass, and to the left down Patterdale and over Brotherswater to Angletarn Pikes and Place Fell, Great Mell Fell on the far side of invisible Ullswater, the High Street ridge and even the Pennines beyond. Behind you the cliffs of Dove Crag are in shadow and over Little Hart Crag is St. Sunday Crag.

Well before you reach the summit plateau of Red Screes, you can look back to Striding Edge and Helvellyn and along from Crinkle Crags to Bowfell, the Scafells and Great End. Through the cross-wall, the path takes you straight on uphill but, when you reach a patch of red shale, you can easily bear left to the rocky outcrops on the skyline, the summit at 2541 feet.

The views from those outcrops around the trig. point are stupendous, especially the view along the shadowed cliffs of Dove Crag, Hart Crag and Fairfield to Helvellyn; down Patterdale and over Brotherswater to a glimpse of Ullswater; down into the Kirkstone Pass and over to the curving back of High Street, cairn-crowned Thornthwaite Crag, flat-topped Harter Fell beyond, and round to the triangle of Ill Bell. Across the summit tarn are the Scafells and the Coniston range, then come Conistonwater and a superb view over Windermere and a golden Morecambe Bay.

Having gorged yourself on the panorama, the reflection of blue sky and whispy cloud in the tarn, and lunch perhaps, turn south, away from Patterdale, to follow the ridge southwards, via a series of large cairns. The Kirkstone Pass Inn will be down, well down, to your left and the view of Conistonwater, Morecambe Bay, Blelham Tarn and Windermere, lit by a bright sun, becomes fantastic.

Path and ridge descend towards the head of Windermere and you go through a cross-wall, which is where I usually seem to be at lunchtime on Red Screes. It's a bit less draughty than on the summit and, when I last sat there, I could look out to my left to the Howgills and Yorkshire Dales beyond the Garburn Pass, over Wansfell to the column of steam betraying the location of the papermill at Burneside near Kendal, and out over Windermere. It was utterly silent once the Black Arrows team of six aerobatic ravens had finished their wing-swishing display.

The path keeps, I am pleased to say, to the right of the wall round the cliffs on the left before the cairn on Snarker Pike. Then you can look to the right over Rydal Water and Grasmere, across to the Langdale Pikes with Lingmoor and Little Langdale to their left, and over the rooftops of Ambleside, now the descent steepens.

Gentle descents are followed by steeper ones and you should not take too seriously Wainwright's comment that the descent "is so easy a saunter that the hands need to be taken from the pockets only once, to negotiate a stile". But you do need to find that stile. It's down to the right near the corner of the walls when you reach the well-built cross-wall. Over that ladder-stile, keep on near the remains of the wall on the right. Then, as wall and path curve left, there is down to the right a view of your outward route up Scandale.

Shortly after the next ladder-stile (post-Wainwright, it would appear), the path runs between walls. Continue gently descending between them, through the wicket-gate ahead and on between the walls, with Windermere looking close now. After a fine view of Rydal Water with the Langdale Pikes behind, the walled path turns left and then right, down to a stile.

Not far beyond the stile, wall and path turn left. As you do too, survey the skyline to the right, of the Coniston Fells, the Crinkles, Bowfell and the Pikes, and descend towards Wansfell until you reach the road. There turn right, minding the traffic as you have further attractive views of Windermere and ahead towards Coniston Old Man, beside which the sun was sinking through bands of delicate cloud. Soon you are on the edge of Ambleside and, at the old church, can turn towards Kelsick Road for a bus or continue down The Struggle to the car park – or wander where you will for sustenance.

11

Pass: Scandale Pass (2)

The Route: Brotherswater – Hartsop Hall – Dovedale – The Stangs – Little Hart Crag – Caiston Glen – Hartsop Hall – Brotherswater

Distance: 6½ miles (with 1700 feet of ascent)

Starting point:
– Cow Bridge Car Park, Brotherswater; The English Lakes North Eastern Area map, map reference 403134

How to get there:

By car – to Cow Bridge car park at the northern end of Brotherswater on the A592 north of the Kirkstone Pass between Windermere and Glenridding.

By bus – to Cow Bridge car park at the northern end of Brotherswater between Hartsop and Patterdale on the Windermere to Glenridding route (summer only)

Dovedale is a secretive valley, concealing its upper section, known as Hunsett Cove, behind the rocky rampart of The Stangs and seeming to allow into its inner recesses below the great wall of Dove Crag only true initiates of Lakeland. Is my prose too purple? Go and see!

For here is a wonderfully quiet route (I learnt it from Wainwright) up to the head of the Scandale Pass. The walk begins at Brotherswater and climbs to Little Hart Crag, at a height of 2091 feet the guardian of the Scandale Pass and an excellent viewpoint and lunch-spot. When I was last there, I met a lost policeman from Derby. Somewhat off his beat, he had ascended to view the lie of the land for a fell race later that day but could not relate the ground to the map. He didn't have the benefit of this book, you see. Together we worked out his route; I hope he completed the race and is not still up there.

Your descent, unlike his, is steeply down Caiston Glen, the

packhorse route north from the Scandale Pass, back to Hartsop Hall and Brotherswater. If the ground is wet, be careful on the rocks as you descend the glen, or perhaps you should avoid this walk in wet weather, as you have to ford Hartsop Beck (shown as Dovedale Beck on the O.S. map) and the climb from the beck to the ridge can be very soggy underfoot.

It's an interesting walk on which you are likely to see few people, an excellent circuit for including the northern side of the Scandale Pass, and it's only 6½ miles long, with 1700 feet of ascent. The descent forms part of the linear route of 7 miles from Ambleside to Brotherswater or the circuit of 10 miles right round Red Screes, both referred to in the introduction to Chapter 10.

Not long after the policeman had asked me the way, a mountain-biker asked me the time; it was all most confusing!

The Walk

In Cow Bridge car park, ensure you are on the west bank of Goldrill Beck, at the foot of the wooded hillside of Hartsop Above How, and go through the kissing-gate in the corner of the car park farthest from the road. Take advantage of the information board about Hartsop Hall Farm and walk along the tree-hung track above the beck and Brotherswater. The last time I did this walk, a cuckoo called and jackdaws chattered and clattered, and a few late primroses were in bloom.

Between the trees, you can see the road winding up to the Kirkstone Pass. To the left is Hartsop Dodd leading up to Caudale Moor, a pattern repeated ahead by Middle Dodd below Red Screes and High Hartsop Dodd below Little Hart Crag. Between the head of the lake and Hartsop Hall, the twin lumps of Little Hart Crag come into view to the right of High Hartsop Dodd, to the left of which is your return route down Caiston Glen.

Beyond Hartsop Hall, with its attractive limewashed facade, continue along the track, keep to the right of the barns, and, at the junction beside the larch copse, take the right-hand track, signed as

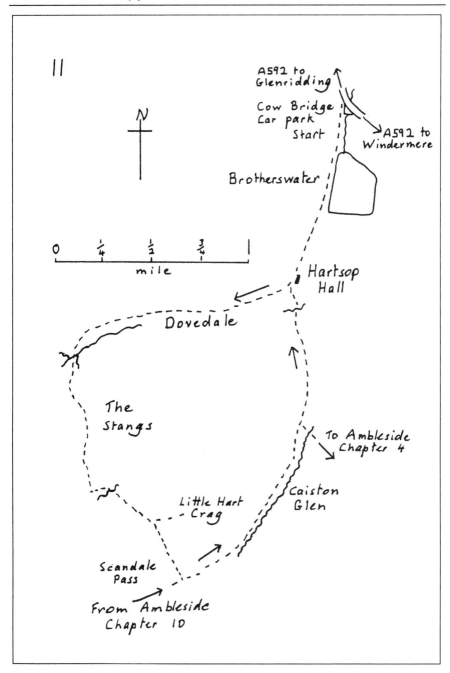

"Permitted fell path" to Dovedale. Now that you have rounded the corner, Dovedale is before you, with Dove Crag at its head.

The track climbs to the arid remains of a leadmine and then, through the gate, becomes a fellside path above a wall. You gain height enjoyably among bracken, wild garlic and a variety of trees. Slowly the realisation dawns that the valley is in two parts; you are now well above the floor of the lower amphitheatre and Little Hart Crag doesn't look too high above you. You leave the main body of trees behind and below you, and the path levels out. Ahead you can see the pass into the upper dale with the path winding above Hartsop Beck, and you can also see that, if you had taken the public footpath from the junction beyond Hartsop Hall barns, you would have had a steeper and more sudden climb than on the route you have followed. As you look ahead, up to the right of Dove Crag is Hart Crag.

Now your walk is enriched by thyme, tormentil and heath bedstraw and by the sight and sound of the beck dropping down Dove Falls. Between Hartsop Above How on the right and The Stangs on the left, you enter Hunsett Cove, the upper valley, where the flowers on the beckside rowan trees looked and smelled lovely.

As you go through the portals of the pass, keep an eye on the fence on the far side of the beck and notice that it begins to veer away from the beck. You need to cross the beck and follow the fence uphill. So, where a sidestream comes in on each bank of the beck, scramble down to the beck, cross it above the left-hand stream and below the right-hand one and follow the faint path up to the fence. There are plenty of rocks on which to make a dryshod crossing of the beck but there are boggy patches on the fellside beyond. When I was last here, they displayed the pendant purple flowers of insectiverous butterwort with its rosettes of greasy leaves.

Up to your right now is the grim cliff of Dove Crag and behind you is the ridge of Hartsop Above How leading up to Hart Crag. This is the tiring bit as you plod up over the grass beside the fence. When the fence turns left, you do, and soon you are high enough to look across to the left to the skyline of the High Street range and then to Angletarn Pikes. Not long afterwards, St. Sunday Crag appears behind you, overtopping Hartsop Above How, and Little Hart Crag comes into view ahead. To its left is Caudale Moor, from where your eye can swing further left to High Street, Rampsgill Head and High Raise, with The Knott in front. And there's the dramatic little cut-away cliff of Stand Crags just to your left.

Beyond that cliff, you follow the fence up to your right and have an aerial view back down Dovedale to Hartsop Hall and Brotherswater and then between Place Fell and Angletarn Pikes to the Pennines. Then the fence turns back to the left and brings you to the rocky cleft of Hogget Gill. Rock steps make it an enjoyable scramble down and up. When you're in the bed of the stream, do look to the left for the view of Dovedale framed by a cantilevered rowan.

The last stretch of the climb is steeply up between fence and stream with impressive views back to Dove Crag, St. Sunday Crag, Stand Crags and Brotherswater. You attain the ridge at a junction of fences with Morecambe Bay stretching away ahead, seen between High Bakestones (with its cairn) on the right and Red Screes on the left. Little Hart Crag is along the ridge to the left and above it are Ill Bell and Froswick, with Caudale Moor, High Street and Kidsty Pike prominent to the left.

Turn left along by the fence, and fence and path will lead you along the ridge, past cotton-grassy tarns, with views of Brotherswater on the left and Windermere and Conistonwater on the right. Then leave the fence and climb the zigzag path to the cairn on the summit of Little Hart Crag for the view down Scandale, past High and Low Pikes to Coniston Old Man and a wide sweep of Morecambe Bay. It's worth going to the north side of the summit as well, for the view of Brotherswater, Hartsop and Patterdale, Stand Crags and your route along the far side of Dovedale. Upstanding between Hart Crag and St.Sunday Crag is Helvellyn with Striding Edge to its right.

Lunch can be in a sheltered spot with a view, perhaps beside one of the little tarns beyond the cairn. Then retrace your steps to the foot of the zigzags and turn left towards Scandale and Windermere, following the path down to the fence and left along by the fence to the wall. Turn left beside that too and you will arrive at the ladder-stile at the head of the Scandale Pass. Those doing the walk in Chapter 10 will come over that stile from the right and will join the walk in this chapter if they wish to descend Caiston Glen.

When you reach the ladder-stile, turn left (or, if you've come up Scandale, keep straight on) to the cairn and follow the path along the right-hand side of the hummock. The path begins to descend more steeply and care is needed in places, particularly if the ground is wet. The route is generally clear, keeping above and to the left of Caiston Beck, but is less obvious in boggy areas where walkers have sought the dryest alternative – with, I suspect, little success. If you do lose the path, you should soon find it again.

It can seem a long way down but the views are a compensation: as you descend and emerge from between High Hartsop Dodd on the left and Middle Dodd on the right, you see more and more of the Hartsop valley and Patterdale, over Brotherswater to Angletarn Pikes and Place Fell, and across the Kirkstone road to Hartsop Dodd. There are attractive falls in the beck and, at one point, a spoilheap from a mine.

"…the surrounding fells viewed across the lake…"

My legs are always pleased to arrive at the kissing-gate in the wall before the field of scattered trees as the steep part of the descent is well and truly over by then. Go through the kissing-gate and, if you now wish to return to Ambleside by way of the Kirkstone Pass, bear right down to the footbridge and turn to Chapter 4. However, if bound for Brotherswater, follow the path between the trees and down to a barn. Keep by the wall to the next barn, beyond which you take the track across the field, between and beside boulders, with a fine view leftwards up Dovedale to Dove Crag on what may have been your outward route.

Continue on the track, over Dovedale Beck and so to the farm buildings, with Hartsop Hall set beside handsome trees ahead. Turn right alongside the farm buildings, go through the wicket-gate on the left and then turn right along the drive to the left of Hartsop Hall. The last section of the route, where the track is beside Brotherswater and Goldrill Beck, is a lovely finale to the walk. Drink your fill of the surrounding fells viewed across the lake before seeking your car or catching a bus from the road beyond the car park.

12

Passes: the Nan Bield and Gatescarth passes

The Route: Kentmere – Kentmere Valley – Nan Bield Pass – Harter Fell – Gatescarth Pass – Longsleddale – Sadgill – Stile End – Kentmere

Distance: 11 miles (with 2700 feet of ascent)

Starting point:
– Kentmere Church; The English Lakes South Eastern Area map, map reference 456042

How to get there:
By car – to Staveley just north of the A591 between Kendal and Windermere and turn north up the road to Kentmere to park immediately beyond Kentmere church or in the field on the left before Low Bridge.

By bus – to Kentmere church on the Kendal to Kentmere via Staveley route (summer weekends only).

The M6 motorway replaced the A6 over Shap for travellers between Kendal and Penrith, but before the Shap road the route between those two towns went up the Kentmere valley and over the Nan Bield Pass to Mardale (Leland, the Tudor travel-writer, went this way in 1540) or by the parallel route of Longsleddale and over the Gatescarth Pass to Mardale.

This walk, a demanding one, enables you to make the climb from the south through the lovely upper Kentmere valley, below towering peaks and steeply up to the Nan Bield Pass at a height of 2100 feet. A rocky climb of a further 400 feet leads to the summit of Harter Fell for great views, before an easier descent to the head of the other pass at Gatescarth, where you turn south down narrow Longsleddale. The tiring bit comes near the end with another ascent of over 400 feet to recross the ridge between Longsleddale and Kentmere – particularly if you're trotting for the bus on a very hot day. That journey from

Sadgill in Longsleddale over to Kentmere is the first stage of the drove road from Longsleddale to Ambleside, the other two lengths of which are followed in Chapters 6 and 7.

The routes to and from the two high passes give a marvellous feeling of following old highways. The two valleys are attractive but very different, with dramatic skylines, and the views from the top of Harter Fell make the sweat sweet – but perhaps the walk should be undertaken only in good visibility.

A logical extension to this walk would, I suppose, be to descend to Haweswater from the Nan Bield Pass and then to climb up to the Gatescarth Pass, to experience the other side of the two passes rather than the summit of Harter Fell, but that would add 3 miles and 1750 feet of ascent to the walk (already 11 miles with 2700 feet of ascent), really rather much. Nor have I included the Mardale – Gatescarth – Harter Fell – Nan Bield – Mardale circuit as a separate walk as there is no public transport to Mardale, but, if you want to do either, it's up to you . . .

The Walk

From the bus stop and car park beyond Kentmere church, walk back towards Staveley and turn left at the east end of the church, up the lane signposted to Upper Kentmere. At the first fork, bear right on the rougher track, winding between walls and past Rawe Cottage.

In a field on the right, four rocks stand like a crude stone circle, and you keep to the right of the farm and along the track beyond. From the crest of a little rise, you have an impressive view of Kentmere Pike and Harter Fell ahead and Calfhowe Crag to the left. Stepping-stones on the left keep you out of the pool on the track and you go through the gap-stile in the wall on the right. Then cross the River Kent by the footbridge, under trees and over the clear water.

On the far bank, follow the path on the left, climbing the rocky hillside to the step-stile in the wall ahead, with a split boulder to the right. Now turn left along the walled track (Low Lane) towards the head of the valley. After crossing a stream, take the green lower track, signed for Mardale, with the exciting Yoke-Ill Bell-Froswick

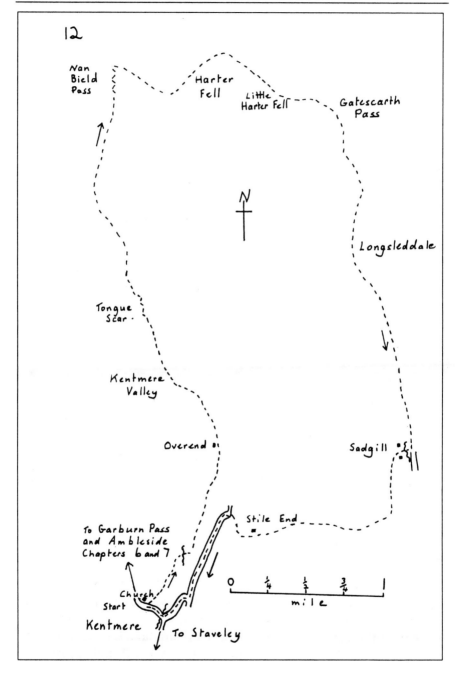

ridge being revealed on the left, and Thornthwaite Crag and High Street beyond.

Your route keeps by the left-hand wall before and after crossing a stream by a magnificent slab of a bridge and does not climb to the farm at Hallow Bank. Keeping a little above the valley-floor, the track brings you to the farms at Overend, with crowstepped barns.

Beside the second house, bear right up the green track, again signed to Mardale. The track follows a terrace along the hillside, with Yoke, Ill Bell and Froswick majestic ahead. It really is a very attractive track which leads you round the hillside, but then it begins to climb to the right of Tongue Scar. The bright golden stars of bog asphodel shone on the boggy ground before the ford with waterfall on Ullstone Gill, a good spot for a stop.

Then go through the gate and up the cairned and worn path and through the bracken. The shoulders of Kentmere Pike and Harter Fell are up to your right and there is a good view back down the Kentmere valley. The gradient eases as you bear right over the shoulder of The Tongue, and Yoke, Ill Bell and Froswick come into view again.

Where the line of the path is less clear (and this is important when you are wearing hot, steamy spectacles), there are cairns to follow, but you are more likely to be looking across to the quarry below Steel Rigg, to Kentmere Reservoir, to Rainsborrow Crag below Yoke, and to Rainsborrow Cove and Over Cove gouged out of the ridge south and north of Ill Bell. You ascend below Smallthwaite Knott, and the three peaks of Yoke, Ill Bell and Froswick are superb. The whole of Kentmere Reservoir comes into view and the head of the Kentmere valley leading up to Hall Cove and the source of the River Kent below High Street.

Then Lingmell End, thrusting forward from Mardale Ill Bell, dominates the scene and you round the corner to see the head of the Nan Bield Pass before you. It looks formidable. The path hardly rises now before its final fling and then, invisible from a distance, an exceedingly-welcome series of well-graded and well-preserved zig-zags greatly eases the climb. Just as you think there can't possibly be much more climbing, the wind-shelter at the head of the pass appears and you're there.

Look at the terrific view behind over Kentmere Reservoir and ahead over Small Water to Haweswater. At last there was a breeze, sufficient to unseat the hat of one of the few other walkers I met when I last did this walk, and our conversation was an excuse for a brief respite in my climb.

Now turn right up the rocky prow of Harter Fell. The stony staircase leads up a rough ridge narrow enough for views of Kentmere to the right and Haweswater and Small Water to the left. The gradient was demanding enough to ensure that the two descending cyclists were wheeling their bikes and not riding them. Cyclists please note – this is not a challenge!

Suddenly, at a cairn, you are on the grassy summit plateau of Harter Fell, with Blea Water now appearing to the left. Keep on as far as the fence, where you arrive at the summit cairn, at a height of 2539 feet. From there, if visibility is good, you can see to the mouth of the River Kent in Morecambe Bay (as you stand not far from its source), Windermere, the Coniston Fells, the heights of the heart of the Lake District gathered round the Scafells and Gable, the Helvellyn range, Blencathra in the north, the Pennines to the east, and over to Ingleborough in the Yorkshire Dales.

Follow the fence to the left, past boundary stones, to the cairn near the point where the fence turns right, south-eastwards. From here you have a full view of Haweswater with the track from the Nan Bield Pass descending to its head. The car park looks a long way down – over 1500 feet, in fact. After the climb, and with that view, here's your lunch-spot, weather permitting.

From the corner of the fence, follow it south-eastwards, descending (with the wiggles of the track climbing up to the Gatescarth Pass visible down to your left), then over Little Harter Fell. Finally, turn left to take the path winding gently and clearly down to the Gatescarth Pass. Your route lies to the right, through the gate, but it's worth a slight detour to the left to look at Harter Crag, the north face of Harter Fell.

Once through the gate, the descent to Longsleddale begins with a slight climb! Then you round a corner and descend, with the length of Longsleddale before you, confined between Buckbarrow Crag on the left and Goat Scar on the right. As the route steepens, it forms zigzags, but more eroded by water than those on the ascent.

The path becomes a quarry track and passes a sheepfold and a signpost to Mosedale and Swindale Head. Continue down the valley. The track, walled and stone-pitched for long stretches, to prevent horses' hooves slipping, descends beside a delectable beck, the River Sprint. Keep peeping over the wall at its falls and dubs, where hot bathers were submerged in an attempt to keep cool, while sunbathers roasted on rocks. After performing a final zigzag, the track reaches the flat-floored valley and continues along its side, with a very different atmosphere from the upper reaches of the dale. In two places on Goat Scar young buzzards screamed for food.

The first habitations, farms across the river, mark your arrival at Sadgill, and here you cross the river by the old stone bridge. On the far bank, follow the track through the gateway on the left and then right before the farm to obey the sign for Kentmere. The track climbs steadily along the fellside, providing good views of less-savage lower Longsleddale.

At a wooden gate, you reach another sign for Kentmere and continue uphill to cross the ridge by the pitched and stony track. The light stone of the little cliff by the stream on the left reveals, I imagine, the narrow band of Coniston limestone between the Borrowdale volcanic rock and the Silurian shales, a weakness exploited by the track you are following. The gradient eases and, at a cairn, you reach the summit of the pass. Now it's downhill all the way as the delightfully easy track swings along the hillside with an increasing promise of the Kentmere valley ahead.

When you reach the buildings of Stile End, there are superb views over and between the old stone farmbuildings, up the Kentmere valley to the trio of Yoke, Ill Bell and Froswick. Then the track swings to the right and back to the left to join the minor road of High Lane.

Turn left along the road and appreciate the final selection of views across the valley to the roughness of the crags below Yoke, dotted with trees and houses, and with the Garburn Pass track climbing the far side of the valley. Pass the end of the track signposted to Mardale (you joined it a little farther north some hours ago) and turn right down the first minor road. This gives you lovely glimpses of the River Kent babbling below you. You arrive at Low Bridge (near the car park in the field) and can turn up to the right, over the River Kent, to reach the church with bus stop and car park just beyond – and a final view of the flat fields stretching down to Kentmere Tarn.

". . . there are superb views over and between the old stone farmbuildings . . ."

13

Pass: Threlkeld Common

The Route: Threlkeld – Guardhouse – Wallthwaite – Lobbs – Old Coach Road – St. John's in the Vale – Threlkeld

Distance: 11½ miles (with 1000 feet of ascent)

Starting point:
– Threlkeld Church; The English Lakes North Eastern Area map, map reference 322254

How to get there:

By car – to Threlkeld on the north side of the A66 between Penrith and Keswick and turn up Blease Road (leading to Blencathra) to the car park in the north-west of the village.

By bus – to Threlkeld church on the Penrith to Keswick route.

The ostensible purpose of this walk is to follow 4 miles of what the O.S. map calls the "Old Coach Road" between Matterdale and St. John's in the Vale, but it may well feel like a pilgrimage of homage to Blencathra's wonderful southern facade. This is because, for much of the walk, that dramatic prospect is in view, but you should not allow that to distract you entirely from other fine views, especially over the great sweep of fells from south-west to north-west or the intimate acquaintance which you make with the northern end of the Helvellyn range.

However, the real object of your walk is that Matterdale-St. John's in the Vale route, which Brian Paul Hindle doubts was ever used regularly by coaches, which would have utilised the route on the northern side of the Glenderamackin valley, through Threlkeld. He thinks it was used for transporting peat and for general cart traffic.

Whatever its purpose, it will take you across the "no-man's land" between the central and northern fells, with a succession of great

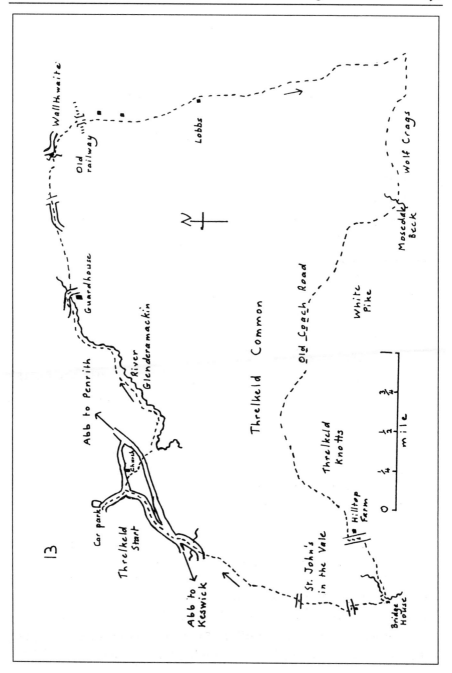

vistas. Before and after the old road are very pleasant stretches of valley beside the River Glenderamackin and St. John's Beck. Because on this walk of 11½ miles (with 1000 feet of ascent), no part of the route is above 1500 feet in altitude, it is a good walk for a day when the cloud is resting on the felltops. But, if the day is wet or there's been a wet spell, the pathless part of the walk immediately before you reach the old coach road will be damp indeed. You have been warned – but squelching feet are a small price to pay for this walk.

The Walk

From the car park in Threlkeld, walk down to the village's main street and turn left to the church. Now, with those who have arrived by bus, take the track, signposted as a footpath, beside the western edge of the churchyard, with the flank of Clough Head before you and High Rigg, the back of Walla Crag, Catbells and lots of exciting fells to the right. You'll see them better later, but this isn't a bad start to a walk.

Before the garden gates, climb the stile on the right and bear left across the field to a stone gatepost and then to a stile onto the main road. Rowling End was now visible over to the right but Causey Pike was still in cloud; Clough Head is dominant ahead.

Cross the road to the fingerpost and stile and keep straight on over the field to a gate and stile by the River Glenderamackin, descending from north of Blencathra. Turn left along the bank and over the footbridge and stile, in a delightful patch of harebells and lady's bedstraw, a foretaste of flowers to come. Now, as you continue along the bank of the River Glenderamackin, to the left you have a fine view of the ravines and spurs of Blencathra. I enjoyed raspberries and masses of wild flowers: vetches, salad burnet, betony, knapweed, meadowsweet and lots of others beside the track beyond the metal bridge. To my right I had the constant company of the rippling river and to the left the great buttresses supporting Blencathra.

Pass the bridge leading to the golf course and continue by the river. As it bends north, you look straight up one of Blencathra's edges and see another in horrifying profile. After two footbridges over sidestreams, the path brings you to a minor road, where you turn right to cross the Glenderamackin by Guardhouse Bridge.

On the far bank, you take the footpath through the gate on the left and over the slab-bridge. Follow the top of the riverbank to a stile in the first cross-fence and then keep on in the same line (gradually bearing away from the river) to a crossing of a ditch, up to a wall and through two gateways to the road. Behind me Hindscarth, Robinson, Red Pike and Grisedale Pike had defeated the cloud but it was still sitting on the Causey Pike ridge.

Turn left along the road, sufficiently minor to have grass in the middle (always a good sign for a walker), with the great mound of Great Mell Fell ahead. It comes as a surprise to see the arches of a viaduct ahead to the right, where the Penrith-Keswick railway line crossed Mosedale Beck.

At the T-junction, climb the stile by the gate and follow the path through rushy fields to another gate and continue to a gate leading to a bridge over Mosedale Beck. Before crossing, look back at the view of four edges ascending to the summit ridge of Blencathra. Across the beck, follow the track to the right and then left between the buildings of Wallthwaite farm and out to the road.

Admire the finely-built gable-end on the far side of the road and turn right to the ladder-stile, from the summit of which there is a good view of the viaduct and Great Dodd. Over the stile, keep along the left-hand edge of the field and then bear right up to a post on the skyline. Now follow the bank uphill to a stile and then slightly right to a gate. Souther Fell is now behind you.

A stile by the gate leads to an arched, iron bridge over the old railway and then, over another stile, you make for the one to the right of Highgate Farm. Over the ladder-stile, follow the waymarks to the next gate and stile and then along the right-hand side of the field, with a superb array of fells to your right.

Climb the next ladder-stile, keep on to another at the top of the field and then make your way through the rushes to the helpful waymarks ahead, towards the farm. Cross a stream and a stile and bear left over two more stiles to Lobbs farm. Latrigg is to your right at the foot of Skiddaw and beyond are Barf and the other fells to the west of Bassenthwaite Lake.

At the farm, lonely and remote, climb the ladder-stile by the gate on the left, turn right over the stream, and follow the path up to the right for a few yards. Aim a little to the right of the corner of the wood ahead to the left. You cross a ditch, a vague path appears in the reedy grass and then there's a waymark ahead. The path is clear now, up to another waymark (don't bear left to the gate near the wood) and gently climbing to a further waymark on the skyline. From there you bear left to a stile by a gate, with the fells north of Souther Fell, around Bowscale Fell, now visible to the north and Great Mell Fell looking much closer to the left.

Once over the stile, turn right and follow the path, always just visible, as it bears away from the fence and then to a stile by a gate in the fence ahead. To your right Skiddaw Little Man and the summit ridge of Skiddaw itself should have appeared and ahead is the rock of Calfhow Pike between Clough Head and Great Dodd.

On the stile, the waymark arrow would have you bear left, but I don't know why it bothers. I kept thinking I'd found a path but then it disappeared, and most bits of this bog seemed as wet as the other bits. The placenames of "moss", "sike" and "beck" warn you what to expect underfoot. I can only suggest that you make sure your boots are well waxed, don't stop too long in any one spot and make for a point between the wood on the left and the prominent red gully on the fellside. The old road is unfenced, so it doesn't matter where you reach it. I arrived near a large, flat rock, an excellent coffee-spot as I looked over to the Pennines. Across a dull foreground was an exciting beyond: Souther Fell, Blencathra, Lonscale Fell and the summit of Skiddaw.

With the Pennines at your back, take the old road towards Clough Head and with Blencathra ahead to your right. It's good to be on solid ground again, striding out as the track marches on below the cliffs of Wolf Crags, across Mosedale Beck, over Threlkeld Common and round the foot of Clough Head, with little ascent to deter you. From the outcrop of White Pike people were casting themselves off on parachutes. A raven cronked in derision:"I came, I soared, I conquered – and without all that expensive equipment." To the right, Cross Fell, highest point of the Pennines, was visible between Great and Little Mell Fells.

When, at about the old road's highest point of 1434 feet, Threlkeld comes into view at the toe of Blencathra, you can make out most of your earlier route along the river, up through farmland and over rough moorland to the old road. Then, as you round the corner, you look over the flood plain between Derwentwater and Bassenthwaite Lake and up through the Whinlatter Pass.

Now the track begins to descend below Threlkeld Knotts and towards St. John's in the Vale. The magnificent massif of Blencathra is ever-present to the right, but it's the view ahead which now demands your attention as it widens southwards with the curve of the old road. Over High Rigg are High Seat and Bleaberry Fell above Watendlath, and then, as your eye swings to the right, come Walla Crag, Dale Head, Hindscarth, Robinson, Red Pike, Ard Crags in front of Sail, Eel Crag and Grasmoor, Catbells, Causey Pike, Grisedale Pike, Lattrigg, Dodd, Skiddaw, and Lonscale Fell on the far side of the Glenderaterra's gash between Skiddaw and Blencathra. As I sat on a rock to eat my lunch, I could even see, in the direction of Whinlatter, Castlerigg stone circle, just to the left of the trees round a white farm.

The track reaches quarry workings and you continue on it, downhill to a gate below a seat. Ahead is tree-topped Raven Crag above Thirlmere and beyond are Ullscarf and Steel Fell. Keep on the track below the quarries and beside the bubbling stream. The rhythmical noise is that of a hydraulic ram – nothing to do with tupping!

The track finally wiggles its way down to the road, where you turn left after noting the signpost to Matterdale, evidence that the old road is open to all traffic in law if not in fact. Your road now leads below the cliff of Wanthwaite Crags and towards the Castle Rock of Triermain. Opposite the entrance to Hilltop Farm on the left, turn right along the track, signposted as a footpath, and Helvellyn Little Man will appear to your left.

Where the track turns left, climb the ladder-stile ahead. Descend the path to the beck and turn left through the gate and along the bank until you can cross the beck by the footbridge near Bridge House. Follow the track to the left and then go over the stile by the gate on the right before the house. Now bear right into the corner of the field with a single tree in front of Blencathra. Through the gap in the wall, climb the stile and turn left by the wall, with a good view to your right of the old coach road's descent, and Blencathra looking tremendous ahead of you again.

". . . Blencathra looking tremendous ahead of you again . . ."

On the road at the end of the field, turn left for a few yards. Note the door high up on the barn on the left and no steps, not a mistake as it's a winnowing-door, opened like the doors on the far side of the barn to provide a through-draught which would blow the chaff away when the grain was being winnowed.

Turn right, at the first signpost, through the second gate. Follow the track through two fields and over the stile into the third, and turn left along the field edge to the next stile and a fine view of

Blencathra framed by trees. In the next field, keep by the line of trees to the road.

Take a few paces to the right and then go through the first gate on the left to follow the left-hand field-boundary, again aiming for Blencathra. At the end of the third field, where drainage works have brought rocks to the surface, you are in a walled enclosure. Go through the large kissing-gate on the right and then not through the metal gate ahead but keeping to the right of the fence and then over the footbridge and through the normal-sized kissing-gate.

The next kissing-gate is obvious, but mind the spring, as it's strong enough to flirt you backwards in your enfeebled state at this stage of the walk. More kissing-gates lead you on towards Threlkeld, and Blencathra threatens to overwhelm you. As you approach a white house, keep to its left above St. John's Beck and a gate will emit you onto the road.

Turn right along this, the old Keswick-Penrith road, up to the new road, right, and then left up into the village, from where you can make out the course of the old coach road on the far side of the valley. Turn left back to the car park or catch your bus from one of the stops in the village. As my bus returned me to Penrith, I could see to my right much of the route of the day's walk, now without physical effort.

14

Turnpike: Ambleside to Grasmere

The Route: Ambleside – Rydal Park – Rydal – White Moss – Grasmere – Loughrigg – Rydal – Fox Ghyll – Ambleside

Distance: between 2 miles (with 250 feet of ascent) and 9½ miles (with 500 feet of ascent)

Starting points:

– Rydal Road Car Park, Ambleside; The English Lakes South Eastern Area map, map reference 376046

– Kelsick Road, Ambleside; The English Lakes South Eastern Area map, map reference 376043

– Rydal; The English Lakes South Eastern Area map, map reference 365062

– Stock Lane Car Park, Grasmere; The English Lakes South Eastern Area map, map reference 339074

How to get there:

By car – to Rydal Road car park on the west side of the A591 (the road to Grasmere) just north of the town centre of Ambleside between Windermere and Grasmere.

– to Stock Lane car park on the B5287 on the south side of Grasmere village and just north of its junction with the A591 from Ambleside to Keswick.

By bus – to Kelsick Road in the centre of Ambleside on the Bowness to Coniston, Lancaster to Carlisle via Kendal and Keswick, Kendal to Grasmere, and Dungeon Ghyll to Ambleside routes.

– to Rydal between Ambleside and Grasmere on the Kendal to Grasmere and Lancaster to Carlisle via Kendal and Keswick routes.

Three roads through history, two exquisite lakes, two of Wordsworth's homes and countless beautiful views are to be found on this walk.

In his book "Roads and Trackways of The Lake District", Brian Paul Hindle reproduces John Ogilby's map of 1675 showing the route of the main road of that time between Kendal and Cocker-mouth, including the length between Ambleside and Grasmere. The route goes through Rydal Park, along the shore of Rydal Water, climbs round the flank of White Moss and descends to bypass Grasmere village. I think of that as the "second road". The "first road", the mediaeval packhorse track keeping to higher ground to avoid the River Rothay, may have followed the drive along which you walk through Rydal Park and certainly is now the bridleway this walk follows from Rydal Mount, round the foot of Nab Scar and across the neck of White Moss to join the second road, the old turnpike, near Dove Cottage. Some parts of the first and second roads coincide with the third road, the current main road. Its new length is a section this walk avoids – the narrow, busy route round below White Moss and beside the River Rothay.

So your route takes you along a drive through the park of Rydal Hall, which, with a little stretch of the imagination, can be said to have been a seat of the Fleming family for 800 years, before following a terrace path behind Rydal Mount, Wordsworth's home from 1813 to 1850, to Dove Cottage, where he lived from 1799 to 1808. Very different in feeling, both those houses of the poet are open to the public. Between them, a diversion onto White Moss will give strik-ing views of Rydal Water and Grasmere.

For the return to Ambleside from Grasmere, I have chosen, out of all the possible routes in the Loughrigg area, the one which keeps closest to the two lakes and the River Rothay, following the southern shores of the lakes as much as possible, the Rothay valley between them, and then the Under Loughrigg road again beside the river into Ambleside – a real low-level walk for when you don't want to be on the felltops.

The full walk is 9½ miles, with 500 feet of ascent, and best started from either Ambleside or Grasmere, but you could begin at either Grasmere or Rydal and circle the lakes but omit Ambleside, for a walk of 6 miles. Or you could walk just the northern section of the route, so as to follow the old roads from Ambleside to Grasmere (4 miles) or even just Rydal to Grasmere (for the terraced path and White Moss), which is a little over 2 miles. Buses link Ambleside, Rydal and Grasmere.

This walk is a bit of a cheat really, for it follows only a short stretch of the turnpike, but it does lead you along rather more of the beautiful pre-turnpike route. And it doesn't involve much ascent, which may be what clinches your choice of this chapter!

The Walk

From the bus stops in Kelsick Road in Ambleside, walk uphill, with the County Library on your right, to the main street, and follow the main street left past purveyors of tempting comestibles and out along Rydal Road. Go past Bridge House, with Stock Ghyll rushing beneath it, and so to Rydal Road car park. Those beginning the walk at the car park turn left along Rydal Road.

As you follow the road towards Rydal and Grasmere, the rocky hummocks of Loughrigg Fell are to the left and ahead Nab Scar, Heron Pike (snowy when I last came this way) and the head of Rydale come into view. Nearer on the right are Low Pike and the ridge leading up to Red Screes.

After the road crosses Scandale Beck, turn right through the pedestrian-gate beside the elaborate carriage-gates at the lodge to enter Rydal Park on the drive signposted as a public footpath to Rydal Hall. The drive follows the beck, impressively full of meltwater when I last came this way (as was the drive!), and provides an excellent view of the western arm of the Fairfield Horeseshoe. Through the gap between Nab Scar and Loughrigg, Sergeant Man, Pavey Ark and Harrison Stickle appeared white below grey cloud and I could look back to Claife Heights above Windermere. As the drive swings left, you can look up to Silver How with Bowfell beyond. Much nearer, Nab Scar and Heron Pike loom over you.

As I entered the trees in the grounds of Rydal Hall, a pink-chested nuthatch was climbing one of the trunks. Keep on the drive as it curves leftwards towards the hall, past the camp-fire site and then, before the bridge, obey the footpath sign directing you to the right. Go through the gateway, left between the buildings and across Rydal Beck, here rushing over rapids. The hall's attractive gardens are on the left and you keep the hall on the left and the teashop on the right.

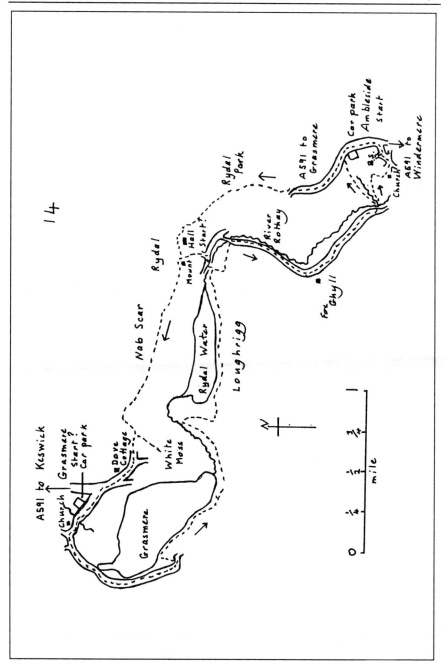

The drive descends to a T-junction, where you turn right up towards Rydal Mount, now on the route of those who have caught the bus to Rydal or have begun at Grasmere and are omitting the Rydal-Ambleside section of the route. The unpretentious house of Rydal Mount is on your left as you go steeply up the concrete track to the right of its car park, above which you turn left along the bridleway to Grasmere, clearly now the old road.

Keep near the gable-end of Rydal Mount and not up to the right to Hart Head Barn. The walled track takes you above Wordsworth's garden; you can peep over the wall and look down on the garden and out to a glimpse of Windermere down the Rothay valley. As you near the end of the garden, you can look onto Rydal Water and across to Lingmoor Fell.

The clear track – it really does look like an old road, doesn't it? – winds its way along the hillside, with the present road rather busier below. On the right is an old trough of stone slabs, no doubt valued by packhorses in the past. You have a good view over Rydal Water's islands to the brackeny flanks of Loughrigg Fell and back to Wans-

". . . The clear track . . . winds its way along the hillside . . ."

fell. G.B.G.'s stone seat is a pleasant place to rest before you enter the wood where, beneath Nab Scar, the track becomes rougher in places. As you reach the end of Rydal Water, you can look ahead to White Moss, with the second road, the turnpike, rising round its flank.

The track becomes the drive from a house on the right and curves round the fellside to cross Dunney Beck. Then the drive turns to tarmac and descends to a roadside pool. The route to Grasmere is straight on but a very fine diversion is to cross the little bridge on the left and ascend along the edge of White Moss. The path is clear out to the head of the promontory, with the lovely view down Rydal Water to your left, Loughrigg ahead and, appearing to the right, Grasmere and its island, with Silver How beyond, Sergeant Man, the Calf Crag-Gibson Knott ridge leading to Helm Crag, and Steel Fell and Seat Sandal on each side of Dunmail Raise with Lonscale Fell (between Skiddaw and Blencathra) seen through the pass. Walk towards the Raise, past the plentiful rock seats and the shelter of an old sheepfold, and you can look down on Grasmere village.

The best route of return to the old road is to retrace your steps to the pool beside the road, where you turn left. The road soon descends towards Sergeant Man, curves to join the old turnpike road, and you continue downhill to reach Dove Cottage with its museum, shop and teashop. At the main road, with the Lion and the Lamb perched up ahead on Helm Crag, cross over into Stock Lane and follow it into the centre of Grasmere. If you are starting this walk from the Stock Lane car park, turn right out of the car park.

Cross over the River Rothay to the church and, according to your priorities, pay homage to Wordsworth at his grave or to Grasmere gingerbread at the Gingerbread Shop, but ensure you turn left opposite the church to follow the road past the information centre. Then take Red Bank Road in the direction of Langdale and Coniston. Follow the road round past the boat-landings and then curving round above the lake. See if you find the attractive view, glimpsed through a wrought-iron gate in an archway on the right, of a stream descending through a garden and under a bridge.

Loughrigg appears ahead and White Moss and Nab Scar are on

the left across the lake. As the road began to climb gently, I had a fine view back to one of the rare shafts of sunlight illuminating the whiteness of the summits of Seat Sandal and Great Rigg, with Grisedale Hause between, before the next hailstorm arrived. A pack of hounds was in full cry somewhere up to my right.

You pass a postbox on your left and then come to a Z-bend, across which you can see ahead a flight of wooden steps just before the road turns sharp right. Go through the gap in the wall on the left and down those steps to follow the permissive path down to the shore of Grasmere. Looking at the house on the left, you can enjoy vicariously a rich Victorian's "get-away-from-it-all" experience, with a view which excludes his mills!

At the shore, look left towards Grasmere village, Helm Crag, Seat Sandal and the back of the Helvellyn range and then turn right, towards Loughrigg and Wansfell. Boulders, benches and beaches may tempt you to rest and savour the views across the lake and up to your earlier viewpoint on White Moss. When you reach the wood, keep to the beach unless the tide is too far in; if it is, take the slightly higher path.

Out of the wood (and preferably out of the water), follow the shore to the footbridge and then keep on the concessionary path beside the River Rothay as it rages through its gorge between the two lakes. At the next footbridge, take the path to the right, climbing not too steeply between the trees to a kissing-gate in the wall at the top of the wood. There you turn left along the fellside, descending beside the wall and towards Rydal Water. Across to your left now are three parallel ridges – Nab Scar and the western side of the Fairfield Horseshoe, Low Pike and its eastern side and, beyond that, the Red Screes ridge.

You come to stepping-stones providing a more civilised stream-crossing than some of those you've had earlier – and will have later – and you can look across Rydal Water to the horizontal wall round the foot of Nab Scar marking the route of the old road. Joined by a wall, the path descends to the edge of Rydal Water. The white house on the far side is Nab Cottage, once home to Thomas de Quincey. A rather wide and deep stream, when I last sploshed through it, is followed by an enjoyable little cliff-contour if the lake's level is high.

As you near the wood at the foot of Rydal Water, the path divides. If you are in a hurry to reach Ambleside, take the upper path, but otherwise keep near the water's edge, through the wood and across the field beyond. On the promontory on the left is a leaning tree of which Heaton Cooper has made an excellent drawing and a charming painting. From here you can look left up the full length of the lake and lift your eyes to Sergeant Man again.

You arrive at the footbridge over the Rothay. To return to Grasmere without visiting Ambleside, cross the bridge, ascend to the main road, turn right along it and then turn left up the road to Rydal Mount, to rejoin the walk's description earlier in the chapter. (Buses will stop near the foot of the Rydal Mount road if you are in need of one.) But if you're bound for Ambleside don't cross the bridge. Instead, just before you reach the bridge, turn up to the kissing-gate in the wall on the right (not to the farm). The path through the wood brings you out on the upper path from Rydal Water, and you turn left down this drive to the Under Loughrigg road at Pelter Bridge.

Turn right along that road, usually quiet and always flat (well, almost), between river and fell. I was not tempted to use the stepping-stones as they were completely submerged by the churning waters. You pass Fox Ghyll with its delightful ogee entrance. The road rises a little and you can look back to Low and High Pikes and Dove and Hart Crags and across to Red Screes, its snowclad summit by now in cloud again. As the road descends, there is a revealing view back to the left of the whole of the Fairfield Horseshoe with Fairfield itself at the head. All the fells from Heron Pike round to High Pike were snowy, but the sun adamantly refused to light them up for a photograph.

The spire of Ambleside church appears over the trees ahead and you know you've not far to go. Across the cattle-grid, turn left over the stone arch of the bridge to the far bank of the Rothay. For the most direct route to Rydal Road car park and Grasmere, take the path straight ahead, later joining Stock Ghyll, along the road to the main road and either left towards Grasmere or right to the car park.

Or, for the centre of Ambleside, having crossed the Rothay, turn right and cross the next bridge as well before turning left beside the white water of Stock Ghyll. Beck and path part and the path takes you round to the right, to public conveniences. There turn left past the church. I recommend turning back to the right and into the churchyard to the doorway at the north-west corner of the church to see the rushbearing mural inside on the west wall. Then take the drive past the east end of the church, along the road ahead as far as Kelsick Road, and there turn left up Kelsick Road to the bus stops, town centre and, if your car is in Grasmere, the continuation of the walk.

15

Turnpike: Kendal to Shap (1)

The Route: Kendal – Bowbank – Otter Bank – Watchgate – Bannisdale High Bridge – Ashstead – Rossil Bridge – Otter Bank – Skelsmergh Hall -Kendal

Distance: between 9 miles (with 1000 feet of ascent) and 16 miles (with 1300 feet of ascent)

Starting points:

– Blackhall Road Car Park and Bus Station, Kendal; The English Lakes South Eastern Area map, map reference 515929

– Kendal Railway Station; The English Lakes South Eastern Area map, map reference 520932

– Meadow Bank, Kendal; The English Lakes South Eastern Area map, map reference 523947

– Otter Bank, Skelsmergh; The English Lakes, South Eastern Area map, map reference 532972

How to get there:

By car – to Kendal on the A6 between Carnforth and Penrith and park in the Blackhall Road car park reached by turning right off Sandes Avenue on the northern side of the Kendal town centre one-way system.

– to Meadow Bank on the northern edge of Kendal just over 1 mile north of Kendal town centre on the A6 to Penrith and park on the old road on the western side of the A6.

– to Otter Bank at the junction of the A6 to Penrith and the minor road to Whinfell about 3 miles north of Kendal and park in the lay-by south of Otter Bank.

By bus – to Kendal Bus Station on, inter alia, the Lancaster to Carlisle via Kendal and Keswick route.

By train – to Kendal on the Oxenholme to Windermere line.

On the 30 or so miles of walking in this chapter and the next, I saw no other walker. The land, though empty of other foot-travellers, was full of interest as I followed the route of the 1753 turnpike between Kendal and Shap, now largely superseded by an easier route of the 1820s, right on the eastern edge of the Lake District.

For the first few miles north of Kendal, the old road and the present A6 coincide, but pleasant field-paths take you through the rolling green countryside parallel to the A6 as far as Otter Bank. From here, where you could begin and end the walk, you can walk the old route in safety, on a variety of surfaces from quiet tarmac road to grassy track terraced along the hillside, hiding from the present road or looking down on it. About half-way to Shap, you turn south and follow unfrequented lanes, tracks and footpaths, largely down the valley of the River Mint, back to Otter Bank, and then, by way of Skelsmergh Hall with its pele tower, to Kendal.

From the northern point of this walk, you look up to the Shap Fells but do not have to climb them as the old road had to, because you turn back south before the high pass. So you are in a land of peaceful streams and farms, of green and sheltered places. But you could continue north into the next chapter and make this a linear walk, as I did, for then you have the excitement of walking as much of the old route as possible and repeating most of a real day's packhorse journey. Kendal and Shap Granite Works, where the linear walk north ends, can be linked by bus from Shap Granite Works to Penrith, then train to Oxenholme and finally bus or train to Kendal.

The complete walk in this chapter, from the centre of Kendal and back to the centre of Kendal, is 16 miles in length with 1300 feet of ascent (in little bits). You can reduce that to 14 miles by parking at Meadow Bank on the northern edge of Kendal (to avoid the walk along the road through Kendal) or to 9 miles by beginning at Otter Bank, where the old turnpike becomes distinct from the A6. Neither shorter variation much reduces the ascent. (The linear walk from Kendal to Shap Granite Works is 13½ miles in length with 2000 feet of ascent.)

The walk in this chapter, and its companion in the next, will be a fascinating revelation to you, I suspect – an old road in a new area.

The Walk

With your back to Kendal's bus station, turn right along Blackhall Road and then left along Stramongate. Keep the Provincial Insurance building on your right, cross the River Kent, pass the occasionally-open Castle Dairy, and you will arrive near the railway station, where you keep on under the railway line. If descending from the station platform, turn back left at the road and under the line.

At the fork, keep left on the A6 for Shap and Penrith. When you have crossed the River Mint at Mintsfeet (which conjures up visions of a local delicacy being used to sweeten the smell of walkers' working parts), beside a rather fine modern house and garden, you know you have nearly escaped from Kendal. There are hints of hills ahead and Benson Knott is up to the right as you continue along the A6. An old length of road on the left leads to and from Meadow Bank, where some of you may have parked your cars; if so, turn north along the A6 away from Kendal.

One field beyond the old road, by the sign for Skelsmergh, climb the stile on the far side of the drive on the left and bear right across the field, aiming a little to the left of the prominent electricity pylon. The field makes a corner ahead and there a wooden footbridge will take you over the stream. Then follow the left-hand field-boundary to stay beside the stream, where bluebells, marsh marigolds and blackthorn were in flower on my last visit. Path and stream diverge and, at the end of the field, with a waterworks building across to the left, you keep straight on through the two gateways and beside the wall on the right. Where it turns right, you keep straight on and over the ladder-stile to the road.

Climb the matching stile almost opposite and bear slightly right into the dip ahead. Then keep the fence on your right and go over the stile in the corner of the field whilst listening to the curlew calling. Stay by the right-hand edge of the field, past a gnarled, ivy-clad ash and over the stile at the end of the field, where you cross the Dales Way.

Keep on to the next stile, again in the corner of the field, and, over that, by the right-hand hedge until that turns right. Now it's on ahead, following the curve of the hill to a gate near Bowbank and then up the farm's drive back to the right, with primroses, violets and wood anemones, to rejoin the A6 at Stocks Mill, with Kendal still visible to the right.

Turn left along the road and then bear left through the gate into the first field and descend the sunken track, which feels old, to the stream. At the bridge across it, climb the step-stile in the wall ahead and then bear left to keep above the valley floor and through the gate in the fence. Now follow the track up the valley to a minor road near Garth Bank. Turn right up to the A6 and right along the A6 for a few paces before turning left into the road for Whinfell, beside the farm of Otter Bank. (Walkers starting from the lay-by south of Otter Bank should walk northwards past Otter Bank and turn right into the road for Whinfell.)

Immediately turn left across the tarmac area and through the gate, now on the route of the old turnpike, with views back to Kendal and, I suspect, if the atmosphere is clearer than when I last did this walk, across to the Coniston Fells. Keep to the top of the field and out onto the tarmac road beyond. The old turnpike, bordered by bluebells and yellow archangel, climbed gently into a welcome breeze. The road leads pleasantly over the hill and past Watchgate Water Treatment Plant, with which I assume the conically-roofed mini-tower is connected. All around are hummocky hills: to the left Potter Fell and the high ground between Kentmere and Longsleddale, to the right Grayrigg and Whinfell, and ahead Whiteside. As you descend towards Watchgate, you look up Longsleddale.

At the crossroads, keep straight on beside the barn and its farmhouse (a café!) and so to the A6 again. There turn right along the not-too-objectionable road for a quarter of a mile, past a milestone and so to the tarmac lane on the left with a sign for Mosergh Farm, by a pitched-roofed building. This is the old road again and you can see it making its way between walls to Plough Farm and beside the wall beyond.

Follow the old road, not turning left for Mosergh at the next junction but keeping on over the beck called the Light Water, with Whiteside up to the left. Beyond Plough Farm (an inn when this was

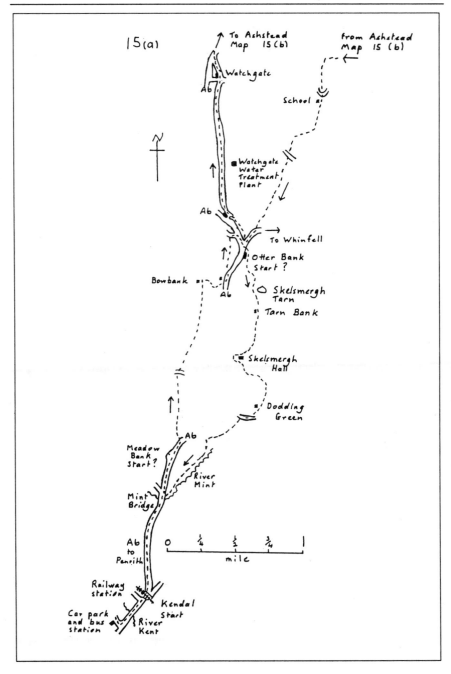

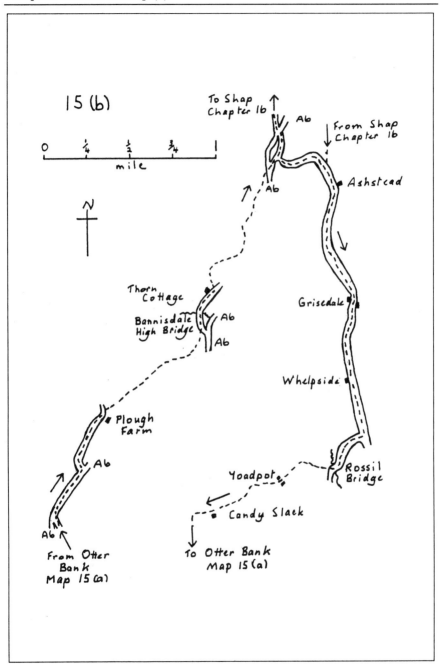

the main road), where the tarmac road turns left, you go through the gate ahead on the bridleway – to begin to feel as though you're really on the old road as it follows first a sunken route and then a well-engineered terrace. It's good and grassy underfoot. Ahead to the right are the four lumps of the Whinfell fells. Look out for the well-constructed drinking-trough (now dry) over the wall on the left.

At the gate beyond the first group of trees, where the track goes from the right of the wall to the left, I had to be shepherded through a dense mass of sheep temporarily penned there in the corner. The air was full of frenzied baa-ing. When the wall turns down to the right to Leagate farm, the track continues ahead, descends, with trees on its right, to cross a drive, and still keeps to the left of the trees. Its sunken course takes you through a gate, between walls, and not quite to the A6. I suggest you go through the metal gate rather than over the mossy step-stile to reach the minor road.

". . . I had to be shepherded through a dense mass of sheep . . ."

Turn left along it, down through the trees and over Bannisdale High Bridge, one of the 17th-century bridges remaining on the old route. One field after Thorn Cottage, turn left through the gate and onto the signposted bridleway heading for the ridge of Lamb Pasture and White Howe on the northern side of Bannisdale, with Whiteside and Capplebarrow on the opposite side of the dale.

Your route follows the track up by the wall and then turns through the second gate on the right and gently round the fellside by the wall on the right, below a bank of gorse and past a thorn on a rock. Over the col, the hills seem to close in round you as you look between Wolf Howe and Ashstead Fell and up Crookdale. Ahead the old road pursues its straight course to the left of the present one – and just to my right a new-born lamb struggled to escape from the afterbirth and stand on its own four feet.

The track descends damply to Kidshowe Beck and rises roughly beyond, following the wall along the fellside and then descending to the A6, with Ashstead Fell now dominant on the right. Cross the modern road, descend to the old one, and turn left along it. If you are making this a linear walk to Shap, continue along the old road and up to the A6 again, but to return to Otter Bank or Kendal in this chapter turn right over the cattle-grid as for Mart Close.

Do not turn left to Mart Close but continue down into the dip and up to the right to Ashstead farm, where those walking from Shap to Kendal come in from the left. This gated road really does seem minor, better suited to packhorses and infinitely preferable to the A6 across the valley. It drops down to cross a sidestream and you follow the valley downstream. The road takes you through the middle of the farmyard at Grisedale Farm, past Whelpside farm, over a cattle-grid and up to a fork. There turn right. Across to the right beyond the A6 is Bannisdale and you have a retrospective view of Ashstead Fell.

The primroses, bluebells, marsh marigolds and wood sorrel were lovely along the road above the River Mint. You cross the Mint at Rossil Bridge, where there is a delightful 17th-century packhorse bridge of stone a few yards downstream.

On the far bank, turn right up the lane to Yoadpot. Bear left at the first fork and turn left behind the barn to reach the farm of Yoadpot, which seems to mean "horse hole" (I have spelled that very carefully!). Go through the gate between house and barn, straight up through the next gate, right beside the house and through the third gate, and then swing up to the left to a fourth gate. From there you can look back to the left for a wonderful vista of the southern face of the Howgill Fells and to the Whinfell ridge.

From the gate, the right of way bears right by a group of boulders and then left by the wall, to keep the hill on your left and bring you to a step-stile in the wall ahead. Over that, bear right and through the gate. Then descend by the right-hand wall to the farm of Candy Slack. As you descend, you can see a ladder-stile beyond the farm. To reach it, pass through the farmyard and the wicket-gate between the garage and the caravan, over one stile and then over another, which much resembles a footbridge, and up to the ladder-stile. However, do not climb it but follow the wall and hedge along to the left, through the gateway at the end of the field, to the left of the house and over the stile to the road.

Turn left along the road (not down the drive back to Candy Slack) and past Selside School. Immediately beyond the school, the road becomes a track leading through gates and across fields and swinging to the right before curving back to the left to reach a road near Poppy Farm. Turn left and almost immediately up the lane on the right, Dry Lane, with the Howgills majestic to the left – and curlew agitated on the right. Keep on the walled road, with Watchgate Water Treatment Plant up to the right and to its right Ill Bell, Froswick and Thornthwaite Crag across Longsleddale. This road, too, soon becomes a track, which takes you past bluebells in abundance and a pond. Over a crest, you see Kendal before you. To the left are the Howgills and to the right the whole of the Coniston range. You descend back to Otter Bank, joining a road for the final downhill stretch.

If your car is parked in the nearby lay-by, turn left along the old road and the A6 to it. To return to Kendal, also turn left along the stretch of old road but then left again through the first gate into the farmyard of Otter Bank. Bear right across the yard and through the first gate and then the second; the route is waymarked.

Now bear right, aiming for the right-hand end of the line of trees.

Go through the gate there and turn left along the edge of the arboreal pond, where I saw my first cowslips of the season. At the end of the pond, keep along by the hedge for a few feet and over the stile on the left. Now follow the hedge to the right until you reach the metal gate and climb the stile beside it. Then turn left along by the hedge to keep Skelsmergh Tarn to your left. Make for the left of the buildings of Tarn Bank and go through the gate onto the lane – where you again cross the Dales Way.

Pass through the gate to the left of the wall round the grounds of the barn (which was being converted into a house when I last came this way) and keep ahead by the hedge. Over the step-stile in the corner of the field, there was a view across to the right to the Coniston Fells, the Crinkles, Bowfell and Great End silhouetted against the late-afternoon sky. Bear left down into the green valley and follow it as it curves to the right to Skelsmergh Hall. On your left as you enter the farmyard is the hall's late 14th-century pele tower. Attached to its far side is the more comfortable 16th-century house.

Having entered the farmyard, immediately turn right through the metal gate. Keep to the right of the large modern building, down the path and steps beyond and through the wicket-gate. Now turn left along the track with an old, slate-roofed building on your left. At the end of that, turn left across the farmyard and, from its far right-hand corner, bear right between the buildings and onto a walled track.

This takes you gently uphill and cattle may well have left evidence of their passing. Where the track forks, keep right to pass beside a pylon and then to swing right along the hillside, with Benson Knott gorse-golden ahead. The track then turns sharp left but you keep straight on to the right of the hedge, over the stile in the wall ahead and through the field-gate beyond. Pass the white house of Dodding Green, where there is a Catholic church (and there are peahens too), stay near the right side of the field, and go through the gate ahead and along the drive. The bank on the right was a glorious display of bluebells.

At the road, turn right, with the River Mint again below you, and, where the road bends right, turn through the gate on the left to follow the fenced path ahead. Keep to the left-hand side of the fields until the wall ends and then swing right, along the edge of the higher ground, to a metal kissing-gate. Now the path leads between river and campsite, past the Thirlmere Aqueduct's crossing of the Mint and along by the fence and trees.

Through the gate to the left of the farmbuildings, walk between the buildings and take the footpath (there's a waymark) to the right of the final building on the left, over the stile on the right opposite its door, and left above the mill tail and river. There is wild garlic to make pungent the last length of footpath round to Mint Bridge, where you meet the A6. If your car is parked at Meadow Bank, turn right; for the centre of Kendal, turn left.

As I sat on Kendal station eating my tea and waiting for my train back to Bolton, I enjoyed not only the food and the rest but also the view to Red Screes, the Garburn Pass, Yoke, Ill Bell and Froswick to the west and the Whinfell range to the north. That's the kind of railway station I like.

16

Turnpike: Kendal to Shap (2)

The Route: Shap Granite Works – Scout Green – Bretherdale – Breasthigh Road – Ashstead – High Borrow Bridge – Packhorse Hill – Shap Granite Works

Distance: 15 miles (with 2300 feet of ascent)

Starting point:

– Shap Granite Works; The English Lakes North Eastern Area map, map reference 565116 (Most of the walk, however, is on The English Lakes South Eastern Area map.)

How to get there:

By car – to Shap Granite Works 2 miles south of Shap on the A6 between Kendal and Penrith and ½ mile south of the junction of the A6 with the B6261 from Junction 39 on the M6. There is a lay-by opposite the entrance to the granite works and another just south of the A6/B6261 junction.

By bus – to Shap Granite Works on the Penrith to Shap Granite Works route.

The northern stretch of the former Kendal-Shap turnpike is very different from that in the previous chapter, for it is over bare, bleak upland, crossing Borrowdale and ascending out of Crookdale by a zigzag with, on the zag, a still-clear shelf along the hillside, where the work of the turnpike-builders is unmistakable. It climbs to a summit about 80 feet above the present summit of the A6 before descending over moorland to Shap Granite Works, which needs to be seen to be believed. So go and see it!

The walk along the old road is the second half of the route in this chapter, for you begin by walking south. You start by making your way through the middle of the granite works to the West Coast Main Line's Shap summit at 916 feet above sea level. There are moorland, plantation, rhododendron thicket and the pleasant valley of Birk Beck, with impressive views to the Howgills, before you turn west up Bretherdale and climb the high pass of the Breasthigh Road (at over 1430 feet almost as high as the turnpike's summit) on an old track which then drops steeply into Borrowdale. Below the slopes of Ashstead Fell you turn back northwards towards Shap again. I think it's marvellous country, and how fortunate that the builders of the A6 didn't choose the Breasthigh pass as their route.

The circuit from Shap Granite Works is one of 15 miles with 2300 feet of climbing, most of it in the ascent out of Bretherdale and that out of Crookdale. I walked this chapter and the previous one as two linear walks rather than circulars, as I'm not dependent on a car! Although the 16½-mile route – with 2400 feet of ascent – from Shap to Kendal (the first part of this chapter and the second part of the previous one) does not follow any of the old turnpike, it really is a super walk and can be highly recommended. Public transport links between Shap Granite Works and Kendal are described in the previous chapter.

While the Lake District to the west is busy with footpath-eroding walkers, try venturing over here to the east now that you've reached the end of the book – but not, I trust, the end of the road.

The Walk

Enter Shap Granite Works by the main gate, keep to the right of the weighbridge and then turn right along the level road, to the right of the retaining wall. Do not go up the rising track on the left. At the end of the buildings on the left, bear left to cross the railway siding by the level crossing or the footbridge (depending on whether a train is in residence) and then take the fenced track up to the right. The works seems less dreadful in this direction than on your return.

Go through the metal gate at the top of the track, into the field, and now bear left over the hill and down to the railway line. You reach the West Coast Main Line near the sign for Shap Summit. Turn right along by the railway cottages and the line, with the Howgill Fells ahead. Keep above the line and the trees and through the gate ahead, from where there is a fine view of the Lune Gorge with the

Howgills to the left and the Shap Fells (over which you will be climbing) to the right.

Do not go over the footbridge across the line but keep along the right-hand side of the hummocks until you reach the plantation. Turn right beside the fence and wall round it and go through the gate on the left just before the pylon and the bend in the wall. Turn right along the far side of the wall and, when level with the stile on the other side of the wall, bear left into the plantation.

Persevere for a few yards even if you think there is no path and a more obvious passage through the trees becomes apparent. Have faith and keep on as straight a course as you can until you reach a track. Turn right for ten paces or so and then turn off to the left into the trees again, the beginning of the path marked by a little cairn. I added a stone to it and you might like to do the same for the benefit of future travellers. Again persevere and your efforts will be rewarded by arrival at a stile in a fence.

Over it, you advance with a wall on the left, but, after only a few paces, climb the stile on the left to enter tunnels of rhododendrons in a mysterious spot which makes you think you are in a secret Victorian garden. Continue along the path above the stream until, by a cascade, you arrive at a shelter with what appears to have been a drinking-fountain – the saline Spa Well. Wainwright says the water tasted like "train smoke mixed with bad eggs", so obviously it was highly therapeutic.

From the well, take the path beside the beck and keep to the left of the buildings of Shap Wells Hotel. Ascend its drive towards the railway and M6. Over the cattle-grid, look left to the Queen's Monument, Britannia on a column commemorating Victoria's accession to the throne, and then bear right along the track beside the wood, with another fine view of the Howgills and Lune Gorge. When the track turns right to a gate, keep straight on across the sidestream, where there are the remains of a stone bridge, up the track just to the left of the trees, and through the gate ahead. Now keep straight on over boggy ground to the far corner of the field, to arrive at a bridge under the railway.

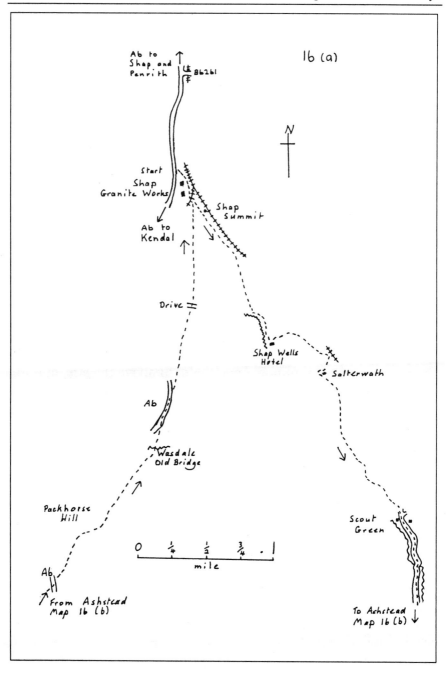

16 (a)

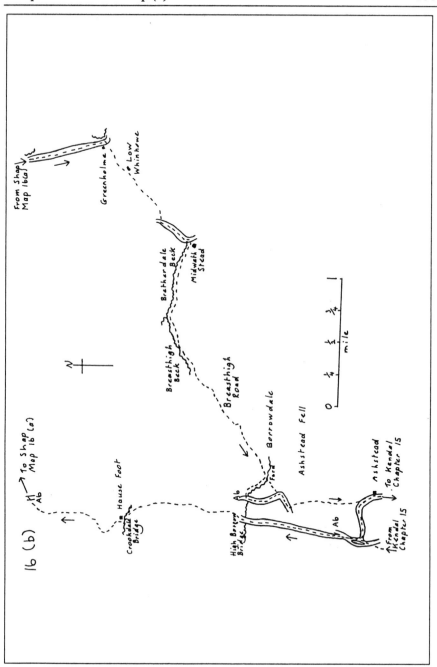

Turn right, away from the bridge and along the drive to Salterwath farm. Enter the farmyard by the first gate, pass the farmhouse and turn left through the metal gate and along the top of the wooded cliff in a delightful spot above Birk Beck, with the Howgills ahead again.

After only a short distance, veer left away from the stream and towards the far corner of the field where, a little to the right of the gate, you climb the step-stile in the wall. From that stile, rejoin the top of the riverside wood and follow it to the stile in the next cross-wall (the stile is on the brink of the drop to the beck) and you look straight up Langdale into the heart of the Howgills. This is a good stretch for train- and lorry-spotting.

Stay with the wall and fence ahead and then turn left to the ruined bank-barn. Go to the left of the barn, right on its far side, through the gate to its left and turn right along the grassy track, which then curves left parallel to Birk Beck. The track becomes more obvious and leads you down to a farm drive, where you turn left as far as the road junction. Here is curlew country.

Turn right along the road and through the hamlet of Scout Green. Do not cross the beck by the footbridge beyond the barns but keep on the road, beside the beck with its bed of limestone slabs and boulders and primroses on its banks. When the road turns sharp right across the beck, so do you. Stay with road and stream until you and the road climb for a view of Tebay set below the Howgills, with Mallerstang Edge across to the left. Ahead are the fells to the north and south of Borrowdale, but your interest should be centred on the valley with the trees across to the right, for that is Bretherdale, your route.

At Greenholme you rejoin Birk Beck, but only very briefly, for, in this pleasant hamlet, you turn right, after the Methodist church and the telephone box and opposite the bench, to go through the gate and up the farm drive. Now you have turned your back on railway and motorway and are heading into the hills. Keep to the right of the buildings of Low Whinhowe and up the track beyond. It swings left but you keep straight on uphill, up the hollowed green track to the left of the small building.

When you reach the end of the field, go through the gate and up the field to the left-hand end of the wall ahead to cross the track from ruined High Whinhowe. Now bear slightly right to the gate in the top of the field and up the track to the next gate. From there the track continues across the final field to the road, down which you turn left. As you descend, ahead is the wooded valley of Corkham Beck and to the right is Bretherdale, with your route going up its left-hand corner. The road drops you steeply down to Midwath Stead Farm (a warning of the climb to come?) and you turn right over the beck to follow the lane up the dale.

Violets, primroses and marsh marigolds dot the banks of attractive Bretherdale Beck which, with its limestone bed, might be in the Yorkshire Dales; you haven't taken a wrong turning, have you? There is an island which might make a good spot for your lunch, but perhaps you should wait until you've reached the summit of the pass.

Where the lane turns right over the bridge shortly before Bretherdale Head farm, you go up the walled track on the left beside Breasthigh Beck. The stony track of the Breasthigh Road follows the beck up the side-valley, climbing gently at first but then more steeply. Here I watched a buzzard being mobbed by a pair of crows. The track turns right to cross the stream before the barn, another track joins it, and you follow the uphill track to the right of the wall. Then the track swings to the left and continues to ascend by the wall. You keep beside the wall until it turns down to the left; the track keeps on, clearly and purposefully, uphill. Do keep looking back at the views across to the distant Pennines.

Once through the gate, you are not far from the summit of the pass and you can look back to the masts and dishes on Great Dun Fell with Cross Fell to its left, the highest point on the Pennines. Mallerstang Edge is flat-topped to the right as you gaze over Bretherdale. When you reach the grassy ridge-top, lunch may be in order. Ahead are Ashstead Fell and the steep-sided ridge leading left to Whinfell Beacon. The A6 curves round below you and beyond it the ridges climb up to Lord's Seat and White Howe north and south of Borrowdale.

". . . the views across to the distant Pennines . . ."

As the track snakes down the fellside of Borrowdale Edge, in true packhorse-fashion, Borrowdale is increasingly revealed. You go through the gate beside the Thunder Stone (sounds ominous but there was no threat when I was there) and continue to descend towards Borrow Beck and the A6 with upper Borrowdale beyond. At the gate beside the stream, ford Borrow Beck if you can and ascend the track on the far bank. (I had no difficulty in crossing dryshod, but, if there is too much water for you to do so, you'll need to keep on the track on the near bank and then turn left up the A6.) Back to your right as you ascend is Crookdale, up which you will return to Shap, and slanting up to the right to the pylon-platoon is the actual shelf of the old road – can you make it out?

Pass through the boulder-burdened gate and out onto the A6, cross with care and turn left. Then recross with equal care and go through the first gate on the left, between the powerlines. (If you were unable to ford Borrow Beck, follow the A6 uphill to the left and round the bend to the right and then go through that gate between the power-lines.)

Descend the track along the flank of Ashstead Fell. I could see in the distance, above the coastal hills, Heysham power station and, beyond Lancaster, the Bowland Fells. And I was able to enjoy the gorgeous coconut-smell of the gorse in flower. When you arrive at the road, keep on ahead and turn to the previous chapter for the linear walk to Kendal, but to return to Shap turn back to the right along the road, down into the dip and up to the cattle-grid.

Cross the cattle-grid to arrive at the old turnpike road and turn right to ascend to the A6 (now with those doing the linear walk from Kendal to Shap). Cross the modern road and walk up the old one. It's a pity it now has a tarmac surface, but follow it past Hollowgate Farm, with views down to the right to the modern road on its sweeping curve to the east and the path you descended along the foot of Ashstead Fell on your way south from Shap. From the cattle-grid you can begin to see into Borrowdale to the right and then, over the rise, you see upper Borrowdale to your left. Ahead is your challenge as you look up Crookdale towards the summit of the old road. You can certainly see the very different routes taken by the old and new roads.

Your road swings handsomely down to cross 17th-century High Borrow Bridge over Borrow Beck and to your right you can see, beyond Huck's Bridge, further down Borrowdale. The road takes you between barns; that on the right was occupied by four hugely-horned tups being kept well segregated from the ewes that spring day. Just beyond is another attractive bridge, over Crookdale Beck.

Then it's uphill again and along the floor of Crookdale. Although there are the pylons in the dale and the modern artic.-bearing and caravan-carrying road up on the opposite side of the valley, Crookdale feels a wild and wonderful place to me.

The road comes to an end as you cross Crookdale Bridge at the farm of Hause Foot – significantly named as you can see and will feel. The A6 has been gaining height gradually ever since Borrow Beck, but you haven't, and so you now have to ascend shortly and steeply. So take the track straight up the hill just to the left of the farmbuildings and then left up the rough field and through the gate. My ascent was made easier by the interesting conversation I was having with the farmer as he went to look at his lambing Swaledales: prices are such that it's just possible to make a living as a hillfarmer here where a third of your income is subsidy, but it's vital for the preservation of the landscape.

Beyond the gate, the track turns right and up the hill again before a further turn right takes you towards the powerlines, along an excellently-preserved terrace and through a gate. As the terrace continues, you can look down Crookdale, and then the broad, green track swings left over the hill. Well-drained to begin with, it becomes marshy as it approaches the next gate, with the A6 to the right, and then it crosses a track and continues along the hillside.

It's a gentle ascent now to the soggy summit, the hause, at 1460 feet slightly higher than the A6, before the track curves to the right, its actual course slightly hollowed, reedy and wet. It takes you to a gate and stile leading out onto the A6 well to the right of the plantation. The hills back to the left around Great Yarlside are impressive, the quarry depressive!

Cross the road and go over stile or through gate to follow the very clear track surfaced with chippings. The track is blindingly obvious, neither beautiful to look at nor comfortable to walk on (though I suppose it will weather) as it dips down and then climbs round Packhorse Hill, from where you can look across to the M6. Keep straight on, with Shap Pink Quarry hidious across the valley and a plantation beside the track. Out of the trees flew a large bird of prey, but too quickly for me to identify it.

As the track descends, you can see the successive transport routes together – your old road, the A6, the London-Glasgow railway line and the M6. All it needs now is for the London-Glasgow shuttle to fly over! The trees shield you from the A6, you look across to Shap Wells Hotel, and the track takes you down to a pleasant spot where you cross bouldery Wasdale Beck, which in South Africa would undoubtedly be called the Orange River. It's a good place for a breather near another 17th-century bridge.

The track rises to the A6 and you continue north along the wide grass verge with a view back to your descent from Packhorse Hill and ahead to Shap Thorn, planted as a landmark for travellers. Where the road bends left, go through the gate ahead and along the track – the old route, of course. The track is clear and direct and Shap Thorn is a fine waymark above the plantation. It felt a real privilege to be walking along the old road, totally free of vehicles (and other walkers), with the traffic on the A6 off to one side and the M6 away to the other.

Cross the drive leading to the Shap Wells Hotel and go through the sheep-pens to continue along the track. You can look back to the Howgills and the Lune Gorge, a rather more attractive prospect than the quarryworkings to the left. It's an amazing sight and sound as boulders are chewed, swallowed, digested and defecated by a yellow monster. Indeed, the whole scene as you descend to Shap Works and the railway is monstrous.

Go through the iron gate and down into the works in spite of that. Cross the railway siding by the level crossing on the left (or over the bridge if a train is in) and then bear right along the road with a 20 m.p.h. speed limit, below the retaining wall, and turn left by the weighbridge to the road. There a car may await you or you may await a bus.

Shap Works is fascinating in its ugliness, mesmerising with its rows of pipes, a most odd end to a book of walks. What would travellers along the old road have thought?

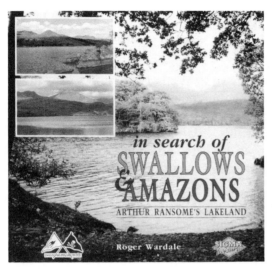

IN SEARCH OF SWALLOWS & AMAZONS: Arthur Ransome's Lakeland

Roger Wardale, whose previous books include Arthur Ransome's Lakeland and Nancy Blackett: Under Sail with Arthur Ransome, has revisited the subject of the Lake District novels. Using the diaries of Ransome and his wife, journals of his friends and Ransome's own notes, Roger has pieced together the fascinating story of how Swallows and Amazons and its Lake District successors came to be written.

Ransome had a lifelong love affair with the Lake District and lived there for much of his life; those periods are recounted in detail, with glimpses of the author, his friendships and romances. "In Search of Swallows & Amazons" is profusely illustrated with both contemporary and archive photographs.

£7.95

TEASHOP WALKS IN THE LAKE DISTRICT

What a great idea! Jean Patefield has selected a super range of walks across the entire Lake District and has combined them with some superb teashops. The walks are all quite short and are perfect for family outings. Each walk has a clear sketch map, interesting photographs and snippets of information about what to look for along the walk – while you're looking forward to scones with strawberry jam!

£6.95

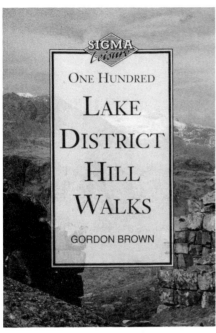

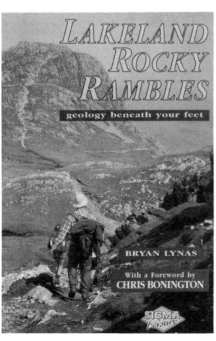

THE LAKELAND SUMMITS: a survey of the fells of the Lake District National Park

Tim Synge

"A really workmanlike job"
MANCHESTER EVENING NEWS . £7.95

FULL DAYS ON THE LAKELAND FELLS: 25 challenging walks in the Lake District

Adrian Dixon

£7.95

100 LAKE DISTRICT HILL WALKS

Gordon Brown

"A useful addition to any walker's library"
WEST CUMBERLAND GAZETTE.. £7.95

LAKELAND WALKING: on the level

Norman Buckley

"A good spread of walks" RAMBLING TODAY. £6.95

MOSTLY DOWNHILL: Leisurely Walks in the Lake District

Alan Pears

"Perfect companion; thoroughly recommended" MENCAP NEWS. £6.95

LAKELAND ROCKY RAMBLES: Geology beneath your feet

Bryan Lynas; Foreword by Chris Bonington

"Refreshing ... Ambitious ... Informative ... Inspiring" NEW SCIENTIST. £9.95

C Y C L I N G
in **The Lake District**

by John Wood

PUB WALKS IN THE LAKE DISTRICT
Neil Coates
£6.95

CYCLING IN THE LAKE DISTRICT
John Wood
£7.95

Other destinations . . .

LOG BOOK OF THE MOUNTAINS OF ENGLAND – Mark Woosey (£9.95)

LOG BOOK OF THE MOUNTAINS OF WALES – Mark Woosey (£7.95)

FIFTY CLASSIC WALKS IN THE PENNINES – Terry Marsh (£8.95)

EAST CHESHIRE WALKS – Graham Beech (£6.95)

RAMBLES AROUND MANCHESTER – Mike Cresswell (£5.95)

YORKSHIRE DALES WALKING: On The Level – Norman Buckley (£6.95)

WALKS IN MYSTERIOUS WALES – Laurence Main (£7.95)

CHALLENGING WALKS: NW England & N Wales – Ron Astley (£7.95)

BEST PUB WALKS – CHESTER & THE DEE VALLEY – John Haywood (£6.95)

BEST PUB WALKS IN GWENT – Les Lumsdon (£6.95)

BEST PUB WALKS IN POWYS – Les Lumsdon & Chris Rushton (£6.95)

BEST PUB WALKS IN PEMBROKESHIRE – Laurence Main (£6.95)

BEST PUB WALKS IN THE NORTH PENNINES – Nick Channer (£6.95)

All of our books are available from your local bookshop. In case of difficulty, or to obtain our complete catalogue, please contact:

SIGMA LEISURE, 1 SOUTH OAK LANE, WILMSLOW, CHESHIRE SK9 6AR
Phone: 01625 – 531035
Fax: 01625 – 536800
E-mail: sigma.press@zetnet.co.uk
Visit us on the World Wide Web –
http//www.zetnet.co.uk/coms/sigma.press/

ACCESS and VISA orders welcome – call our friendly sales staff or use our 24 hour Answerphone service! Most orders are despatched on the day we receive your order – you could be enjoying our books in just a couple of days. Please add £2 p&p to all orders.